In the
Mouth
of the
Wolf

In the Mouth of the Wolf

Rose Zar

The Jewish Publication Society of America
Philadelphia   5743 / 1983

Library of Congress Cataloging in Publication Data
Zar, Rose, 1923–
    In the mouth of the wolf.
    Summary: The author describes her experiences in wartime
Poland and how she survived the Holocaust by passing herself off
as an Aryan.
    1. Zar, Rose, 1923–   –Juvenile literature.
2. Holocaust, Jewish (1939–1945)–Poland–Personal
narratives–Juvenile literature. [1. Zar, Rose,
1923–   . 2. Holocaust, Jewish (1939–1945)–Poland–
Personal narratives. 3. Jews–Poland–Biography.
I. Title.
DS135.P63Z378   1983   940.53'15'03924 [B] [92]   83–4399
ISBN 0–8276–0225–1

Designed by ADRIANNE ONDERDONK DUDDEN

The author gives special thanks to Dr. Eric A. Kimmel,
who worked so hard to put her story into written form.

I dedicate this book to the memory of my parents,
Bela and Herman Guterman,
and my little sister, Pola;
to the memory of my husband's parents,
Regina and Alter Zarnowiecki,
his sister Rachel, and his brother Chaim;
and to our children,
Regina, Harvey, and Howard.

Contents

*If you're ever on the run
and have to hide,
the best place is
right in the
mouth
of the
wolf.*

●

—*Herman Guterman's advice
to his daughter Ruszka*

Prologue

Night. The coming dawn is a knife edge on the eastern horizon as the train rolls south through the forests and fields of central Poland. The train's lights are out, for this is wartime. Behind the blacked-out windows of the third-class passenger cars—the only ones available for civilian travel now that the Germans occupy the country—every inch of space is packed with people and baggage. The darkened carriages vibrate with a restless hum. A hungry infant cries and is quickly stilled. From a compartment come the sounds of laughter and lively conversation. In the corridor a man deals cards. Another passes around a bottle. Some sleep on rolled-up coats or bundles. Others try to. And some, like the young woman in the gray coat with the fur collar, simply sit staring into the darkness, awaiting whatever challenge the new day will bring.

The young woman's name is Ruszka Guterman. She is nineteen years old and already that night, she has looked on the face of death twice. But no trace of fear marks her face nor any hint of the gnawing anguish she feels inside. The people on the train do not even suspect she is Jewish. But I know, just as I also know what she is feeling in her heart on that long night ride south. I know . . . because I was there.

I was that young woman. This is my story.

Escape from the Ghetto

The Jews of Poland knew the end was coming. In fact, we had known for a long time. The casual brutality that marked our everyday existence, the random, senseless beatings and shootings, the murderous forced labor details were all early indications of what the Germans had in store. Added to that was the studied official callousness that set up ghettoes—decrepit districts where Jews were forced to live —drove thousands of people into areas scarcely able to hold a fraction of that number, then denied them the most basic levels of food, shelter, and medical care. With time, according to their calculations, disease, starvation, and simple suicide would write an end to the Jewish people.

But the projections were wrong. Jews failed to die off in sufficient numbers. The extermination program was falling behind schedule. So the Germans, with modern scientific efficiency, developed a solution to solve the problem. A final solution.

My friends and I first learned of it as early as 1940, when an emissary from the Jewish underground in Warsaw came to speak to our youth group. I was seventeen then. We were young Labor Zionists, members of HaShomer HaTzair. Mayer Zarnowiecki, whose father owned a dyeing and chemical cleaning business, was president. He was also my boyfriend. The emissary was a young man whose name is familiar to anyone acquainted with the history of the Warsaw ghetto uprising. It was Mordecai Anielewicz. As we gathered that night for a special meeting, he told us that time was growing short. The Germans were preparing to murder every Jew they could lay their hands on: rich, poor, young, old, men, women, children. It was already too late for our parents' generation and for our younger brothers and sisters. The hope of our people rested on our shoulders alone. Each one of us had to make his or her own decision. He outlined three choices. Though the difficulties were grave, it was still possible for a few to escape to Palestine. Those who spoke Polish flawlessly and whose features were not Jewish could try passing as Aryans. Some, at least, would survive that way. But as for himself, Mordecai Anielewicz explained, the only course was the third: to go down fighting, with a gun in his hand, holding high the honor of the Jewish nation, so that none could ever say we went like sheep to the slaughter. He urged us to make our choices soon, to get our false papers ready, to do our best to purchase guns and ammunition. He promised that the Warsaw organization would try to help us as much as it could.

But the end came sooner than anyone expected, stalking north along the railway. Haggard, wild-eyed strangers appeared telling terrifying stories of how the ghettoes in Radomsko, Sosnowiec, Częstochowa were cleared, and of a camp called Treblinka, where fires burned day and night. Our city, Piotrków, was the next major stop along the railway. It was already the summer of 1942. Its turn was coming.

The first indication that something was about to happen occurred when the Germans surrounded one block of houses with barbed wire. Access to this compound, which came to be known as the "small ghetto," was through two gates. Since such a tiny area could accommodate only an infinitesimal portion of the ghetto's population, it was obvious what the next step would be. They were getting ready for the transports.

Though outwardly life followed its everyday patterns, the air in the ghetto was charged with tension. People began disappearing. Friends, neighbors, people one used to see every day on the street suddenly vanished. Some went into hiding; others crossed over to the Aryan side. Wherever they went, they were gone without a trace. Then the blondes appeared. Girls with strong Jewish features, olive complexions, and dark eyes bleached their hair and became blonde overnight in the pathetic hope that if their hair were yellow they'd somehow be able to pass as Polish and run away. Others, more practical, tried to find jobs in shops and cooperatives manufacturing dresses, coats, shoes. They enrolled in vocational classes teaching tailoring, woodworking, carpentry, shoe repair, hoping that if they had a skill, they might somehow be exempted from the selections. Especially sought after was an *Arbeitskarte*, a certificate declaring that the bearer was an employee of the German military. Equally desirable were jobs in factories and shops working under

German contracts. One ingenious group of young people obtained work cards by collecting woolen rags and reprocessing them for the Army, which purchased the reclaimed wool for uniforms.

Our family, too, made its plans. But, unlike others, we didn't rush about frantically, clutching at impossible hopes. My brother Benek and I, my father decided, could pass as Poles, roles for which our upbringing prepared us very well.

Benek was sixteen. I was eighteen and a half. Neither of us looked especially Jewish. No one in our family did. My mother had beautiful red-gold hair and the bearing of an aristocrat. My father was dark, but with features that were more Russian or Ukrainian than anything else. In our home we spoke Polish perfectly without the slightest Yiddish inflection, a legacy of my mother who was equally fluent in Russian and German. Furthermore, we knew the basic teachings of the Catholic church. My brother once attended a Catholic school and listened in when the priest came to teach the religion lesson. He knew the catechism as well as any Catholic boy his age, and I learned it from him. Most Poles are devout Catholics, and our lives depended on knowing the details of their religion as well as we knew our own.

But we also needed papers. Every citizen had to have an official passport, stamped, containing his or her photograph and the proper signatures. A baptismal certificate was also necessary. These papers had to be carried at all times and presented to the authorities upon demand. This was where my father's expertise came in. In his younger days he had been an artilleryman in the tsar's army. After the revolution of 1917 he deserted and made his way to Warsaw, where he met my mother. When the new Polish republic went to war with the Bolsheviks, my father decided he'd had his fill of fighting. He ignored the order to report for duty and spent the next two years as a fugitive, hiding from the police. His experiences then helped us now. He knew everything there was to know about false papers and shared his knowledge with us.

"All sorts of documents are being sold on the street now, but you can't buy just anything. I know. I was there. I'll tell you what you need. You want a real passport, not some counterfeit that someone printed up in a cellar. You want a real document printed on official paper with the real stamps and the real signatures. Try to get a passport issued to a real person. Then all you have to do is substitute your photograph for his. Stay away from forgeries if you possibly can. That's what the police will be looking for. The real thing will cost a lot of money, but it's worth it. Believe me, it may save your lives.

"Also, you don't want anything in your documents identifying you as brother and sister or showing that you are related in any way. There must not be the slightest connection between you. That way, if one of you is caught, the other will still have a chance to escape. Avoid any papers with the same last name. Avoid any papers with a name ending in '-ski' or '-ska.' Every Jew is becoming a '-ski': Kowalski . . . Rostowski. . . . You don't want any part of that. It's the first thing they'll look for."

Getting false papers was a difficult, dangerous business. It took a long time, and we were extremely lucky to get the good sets of papers we did. I used my underground connections to obtain a blank passport for Benek, one stolen from a government office. I gave my brother's picture to the forger. He attached it and put on the official seal. Benek later filled in his own personal data. He chose as his new name that of a boy he knew at school. Tadeusz Stempien.

My passport gave me even more trouble. Selling false documents was a crime. Those caught were executed. Even outright forgeries were hard to get. Obtaining a real passport was almost impossible, especially since I needed a document whose owner's description matched my own. By sheer luck I was finally able to obtain a passport and baptismal certificate belonging to a woman named Wanda Gajda. Mayer, who was quickly becoming an expert forger, helped me "personalize" them. We steamed off the glue holding her picture and pasted in my own. Then Mayer carefully drew in the portion of the official stamp that cut across the corner of the photograph. He did an excellent job. Anyone examining that document under a magnifying glass would be hard put to say it wasn't real. However, the real problem was that this Wanda Gajda was born in 1913, making her ten years older than I. I couldn't possibly pass as a twenty-nine-year-old woman. Anyone noticing that birth date was bound to get suspicious. What was I to do? Mayer studied the problem and arrived at an ingenious solution. Taking a fine-pointed pen, he carefully change the 3 into an 8, reducing Wanda Gajda to the much more satisfactory age of twenty-four. We were finished. My documents were a work of art.

"But Mayer," I asked, "what about you? Do you have a good set of papers?"

He sighed. "Ruszka, with a face like mine, who needs papers?" We both realized the sad truth. With his strong Jewish features, the best set of papers in the world couldn't save him. He would stay in the ghetto and take his chances.

My parents felt the same way. My mother bought a baptismal certificate, but I doubt she planned to use it. My father didn't have any papers at all. Yet ironically they both had an excellent chance to survive.

In my mother's case, her flawless command of the Polish language and her self-assured manner would enable her to blend in easily once she was outside the ghetto. As for my father, he was bold, resourceful, daring, and already familiar with the intricacies of life as a fugitive. In short, they both could have passed were it not for my sister.

Polcia was six years old, the worst possible age: old enough to talk, but not old enough to understand the situation. Furthermore, she stood out. Her huge dark eyes and blonde hair were a striking combination. People loved to talk to her on the street, and she wasn't shy about answering. What if someone asked her to say her prayers? She was too small, and there was too little time to teach her everything she had to know. My parents' chances with Pola were nil. Rather than abandon her, they chose to remain in the ghetto. But Benek and I were going!

My father had reservations about Benek being on his own. Perhaps he was still too young. So instead he arranged a job for him in a plywood factory manufacturing prefabricated buildings for the Army. When the final selection came, Benek would go to the factory, my parents would go into hiding, and I would leave the ghetto.

But where would I go? Again, my father thought of everything. Some months before, we learned of an old couple named Banasz living on the Aryan side. Mr. Banasz, it turned out, was a converted Jew, a fact he had managed to keep secret for years. But now, with the Germans forcing even converted Jews to move into the ghetto, my father was able to work out an agreement. Mr. Banasz would live with us. In return we would use his apartment outside the ghetto as a depot for storing property and valuables, and also as a safe haven should one of us slip over to the Aryan side. Not that we had any illusions about Mrs. Banasz. The frightened woman quickly regretted ever having gotten involved. But so long as her husband was living with us, we didn't have to worry about her turning us in.

When word came that the action was coming, my sister Polcia was to run to the Zarnowieckis' house and warn Mayer's sister Rumka. She and I would immediately take our bags, sneak out of the ghetto, and go to Mrs. Banasz. My suitcase was packed and ready. It contained a change of clothes, sweaters, underwear, personal items, and, hidden beneath everything, a silver dinner service: a negotiable item in case of emergency. Rumka had three valises bulging with sweaters, men's suits, bundles of dyed wool in every color, and several valuable antiques, including an exquisite gold watch presented to her father by a wealthy baron and a solid silver Hanukkah menorah, a large, heavy piece. It was far too much baggage for one person to carry, so she brought the suitcases over to Mrs. Banasz's apartment ahead of time. The plan called for Rumka and me to spend the night there and catch the train for Ostrowiec in the morning. Ostrowiec was a small farming town in southeastern Poland. Mayer's uncle lived there. According to Mr. Zarnowiecki, he knew the peasants quite well and would help us find a safe place to hide out in the country.

By now rumors were flying like grasshoppers. The air was charged with terrified anticipation. Someone had seen SS men—elite Nazi troops—and their Ukrainian auxiliaries coming to surround the ghetto. The final action was scheduled for tonight . . . tomorrow . . . the day after tomorrow. The first time we heard these rumors, I grabbed my suitcase and hurried to Mrs. Banasz's apartment, where I spent the night. Nothing happened, so the next morning I returned home to find Benek just coming back from the plywood factory. As soon as we entered the house, we saw that something was bothering our father. He was thinking.

"No," he finally decided. "It's silly to take chances. I don't trust those Germans. Benek, forget about the plywood factory. You have your papers. The next time we hear something, you go with Ruszka to Mrs. Banasz, too."

So we did—several times. But each proved to be a false alarm. Benek, Rumka, and I were getting tired of hopping back and forth. In the future we decided to wait until the last possible moment. Then, if it appeared that something was really about to happen, we'd run. But after still another false alarm, we changed our plans.

"Forget about Mrs. Banasz," my father said. "Don't spend one extra minute in this city. When the warning comes, all three of you go straight to Ostrowiec." He even worked out a plan for getting us on the train. Not many people go to a small town like Ostrowiec. It would be very suspicious for three people to suddenly show up at the Piotrków station on the night of an action wanting to buy tickets there. It was better for us to buy tickets for different points, split up, and arrange to meet later on. According to my father's plan, only Benek would buy a direct ticket for Ostrowiec. I would buy my ticket for Koluszki. Koluszki was the main terminal in central Poland. I would take the train to Koluszki, leave the station, buy my ticket for Ostrowiec, then come back in. As for Rumka, she was supposed to walk the five kilometers to Moszczenice, a little town farther along the railway, buy her ticket to Ostrowiec at the station there, and board the train when it arrived. She arranged for the son of one of her father's Polish employees to carry her bags and, more important, go into the station and buy her ticket for her. This was all admittedly roundabout, but if everything went well, we would be together on the same train bound for Ostrowiec by the time it left Koluszki.

On the evening of October 13, 1942, a girl I knew stopped by the house. Her father was well known for having connections with the police.

"It's tonight," she whispered. "They're coming tonight to surround the ghetto. The action is scheduled to begin this evening."

My father overheard. "What? Who told you that? Did your father tell you?" The girl became frightened and tried to take her words back.

"I didn't really hear anything. I was just kidding. It's only a rumor."

But my father knew better. He sensed danger at once. Throwing on his coat, he went out to talk with the girl's father. He wasn't gone long.

"I don't like this at all. I can't get a straight answer," he said when he came back. "No one knows anything. It doesn't look good. We better not take chances. Ruszka, Benek, go get your things. Polcia, run over to the Zarno-wieckis and tell Rumka to leave for Moszczenice at once. She has to be at the station on time." My little sister ran out the door as my father handed me my suitcase. "Now go at once! Don't waste any time!"

Benek changed his mind at the last minute.

"Papa, let me stay. I'll be all right here. Let me stay with you."

"Don't argue! Go!" my father ordered, shoving us out the door. We left in such a hurry that Benek forgot to take his suitcase.

It was the beginning of winter. An icy wind cut through our clothes as we scurried along the alleys, clinging to the shadows, making our way to the secret underpass that would take us over to the Aryan side. We arrived at the railway station shortly before eight and bought our tickets just as we planned: mine for Koluszki, Benek's for Ostrowiec. We hoped the wait wouldn't be long. A train station is a dangerous place for someone on the run: well lit, few exits, and well patrolled by gendarmes and secret police. Our train was scheduled to arrive at 8:10. We sat down on a bench to wait.

At 8:05 we heard an announcement. The 8:10 train was canceled. The next train to Koluszki would arrive at 4:00 A.M. That news was like an iron trap snapping shut on us. What were we to do? We couldn't go home, and we couldn't check into a hotel without showing our passports to the desk clerk. His first question was sure to be "Why are you renting a room when your passports say you live here?" But at the same time we didn't dare wait in the station. That was sure to attract attention. What were we going to do?

As we sat trying to think of something, another train pulled in. "Come on, let's go," I said to Benek. We mingled with the passengers getting off and followed the crowd outside.

Across the street from the railway station was a large park. Nearby were a number of rooming houses where the city's prostitutes worked. But since the Germans had reserved all the hotels for their own use, such rooming houses were often the only places where respectable people could find a bed for the night. We assumed the owners of these places didn't examine papers too closely or ask many questions, so we decided to give them a try. Down the street we went, knocking on one door after another.

"Could we rent a room for a few hours? Our train doesn't leave till four."

The answer was always the same.

"No."

"Sorry."

"We're full up."

By now it was ten o'clock and close to curfew. We couldn't risk staying on the street much longer, so we crossed over and went into the park. It was pitch black. All the street lamps were out because of the blackout. As Benek and I looked for a place to hide, I remembered a bit of advice my father once gave me: "If you're ever on the run and have to hide, the best place is right in the mouth of the wolf. If the police are looking for you, hide in the police station. Hide in the policeman's house or, better, under his bed. Hide in the most obvious place you can, because that's the one place they never look."

A long, winding path led deep into the park, but we didn't take it. Instead, remembering my father's advice, I found two bushes growing side by side right next to the street. Benek took one and I took the other. With a whole park to hide in, it would be hard to find two more obvious places than that.

We lay there an hour . . . two hours. A cold rain began to fall. Suddenly we heard voices. Two German gendarmes were coming up the street, shining their flashlights into dark corners. Huddled in the bushes, we overheard their conversation. They were going to search the park. Being so close to the railway, it was a good place for saboteurs to hide. They turned in at the gate and followed the path to the point where it forked. One branch led deeper into the park while the other ran parallel to the street, right by the bushes where we were hiding. We didn't breathe. If they came this way, they'd catch us for sure.

But they didn't. My father was right. They went the other way. By now we realized that the park was not as safe as we thought. "Let's go," I whispered to Benek as soon as the gendarmes were out of sight. We went back across the street to take our chances in the railway station.

It was very late. The Radom-Częstochowa train had just pulled in. We mingled with the passengers getting off, and as the crowd began to thin I noticed a railway worker walk by carrying a kerosene lantern. He looked tired, as if he were just coming off duty, but he had a kind face. Somehow I felt I should approach him. So I did.

"Excuse me, Mister. Do you know any place where my brother and I could spend the night? We just heard that our train won't be leaving till four. It's against the law to be on the street, and we have nowhere else to go."

He studied me thoughtfully, then said, "Did you just get off that train from Częstochowa?"

I said we had.

He frowned, thinking it over. "Okay, come with me. I have a place. You can stay there."

We followed him to a large apartment building on a side street just off Piłsudskiego Street, Piotrków's main thoroughfare. He unlocked the front door, let us inside, and then up three flights of stairs to his apartment. Opening the door, he motioned us to go in. He turned on the light. Benek and I found ourselves standing in a warm, freshly scrubbed kitchen with copper pots and pans gleaming brightly from their hooks on the wall. A wooden chest filled one corner. The railway man invited us to sit down, then asked, "When does your train leave?"

Escape from the Ghetto

"Four o'clock," I replied. "Maybe four-thirty if it's late."

He took an alarm clock and set it. "You can sleep here in the kitchen, on the chest if you like. I'll get you up on time." In the next room we heard a baby cry and a woman's voice asking, "Jan, what's going on? Who are you talking to?"

"It's nothing," he said. "Nothing at all. Go back to sleep." Then, taking the key, he locked the front door from inside and went into the other room.

A chilling thought raced through my mind. "He knows! He knows we're Jewish! And now he's locked us in so he can turn us over to the police!" What were we to do? There was no way out, no place to run. We were trapped. All we could do was wait. And so we sat up that whole night—mouths dry, hearts pounding, clutching each other's hand so tightly it hurt—awaiting the disaster that would certainly come in the morning.

Just before four, the bedroom door opened and the railway man emerged. "Time to go," he said. "Get your things. I'll take you down."

"No need for that!" Benek and I blurted out at once. "Just open the door. We'll find our way down ourselves."

No," he insisted. "I'll have to let you out the front. I don't want the janitor to see you."

He took us downstairs and let us out the front door. But just before going back inside, he hesitated. I noticed his hands were trembling.

"My God!" he suddenly said. "What they're doing to your people! I saw it. I just got off a train in Częstochowa. I can't take it!"

He knew. He worked on the railroad and saw the deportations with his own eyes. What was being done to the

Jews horrified him. That was why he took pity on us. Our secret was safe.

"God be with you," he said. Then, just before going inside, he gave us some advice. "Girl, you're gutsy. You have nerve and that's good, but I could spot you as a Jew a mile away. Not your brother, though. He blends in. No one will ever suspect him unless they see you together. My advice is keep apart. Don't travel together. Don't let anyone know you're related. A single Jew can get by. Two, never!"

It was excellent advice, coming from a gentile. I thanked him over and over and asked how much we owed for the night.

"Nothing," he said. "You don't owe me a thing." I tried to give him ten zlotys, but he wouldn't take it. "No. You keep it. You're going to need it a lot more than I will."

I reached for his hand and kissed it, for there was no other way of expressing the great flood of gratitude I felt. In a world of enemies, this man—a total stranger—had given us our lives.

"Benek," I said to my brother as we walked back to the railway station, "we're going to make it. Someone's watching over us."

I was sure of it.

The station was packed by the time we arrived. Travel by train during the war was an adventure. The Germans automatically reserved several cars for themselves. There were only a few places left, but the ticket sellers went on selling tickets as long as there were people willing to buy them.

The result was a pushing, shouting mob struggling to get on board the train to Koluszki. Bundles and people were everywhere. I told Benek to stay close behind. Together we pushed and shoved our way forward to exactly the right spot, so that when the crowd surged forward to board the train, it would carry us with it. We had to fight for our places, but we got them. Then we waited, with the peasants, the businessmen, the mothers and squalling babies, the black marketeers, and all their satchels, suitcases, and towering bundles.

At 4:15, with a shriek of its whistle and a great rumbling of iron wheels, the train rolled into the station. Everyone in the crowd grabbed his or her belongings and got ready to lunge forward at the first signal to board. The trainmen threw open the doors and let out, not ordinary passengers, but rank upon rank of SS auxiliary police, Ukrainians and Lithuanians in black uniforms and boots, brandishing guns and rubber truncheons. There were hundreds of them: laughing, jolly, a few drunk and tipsy. They looked like young men going to a party . . . or coming back from one. A deadly chill swept over me as I glanced from one handsome, merry face to another. This was the living wall sent to surround our ghetto. My own executioner was there, I knew, finding his place among the lines now rapidly forming. Was I looking at him now? My heart turned to ice. I drew back, but the crowd pushed me forward. They were cheering, as they had been, ever since the first black uniform emerged from the cars.

"Ho, ho! Our poor little Jews!" they cried. "They're sound asleep in their beds. They don't know what's in store for them tomorrow, poor little Jews!" And they laughed. "Sleep well, little Jews. Tomorrow is your day!"

The train was empty now. The trainmen gave the signal to board. The crowd began to move. Suddenly I wanted to run. I didn't want to be here. I wanted to go back, back to my home, to my room, to my mother and father. I turned around to Benek and said, "What are we doing here? Let's go home."

He looked at me as if I'd lost my mind. Then his eyes blazed and he shoved me forward so hard I scraped my shin against the iron steps leading up to the cars. The surging crowd carried us forward and onto the train.

The station at Koluszki was an immense cavern. Every fifteen minutes trains arrived from all parts of the country. Crowds of people were constantly coming and going. As soon as we pulled in, Benek got off and sat down to wait for the train to Ostrowiec. I left the station with the other passengers. I walked around to the other side of the building and came in through another gate so as not to arouse suspicion. I bought my ticket for Ostrowiec and sat down to wait for the train, too.

We had a long wait. Every fifteen minutes either Benek or I would get up and walk around. To the casual observer we were just stretching our legs, but what we were really doing was combing the station for Rumka. Where was she? Her whole plan was undoubtedly disrupted by the cancellation of the eight-o'clock train, but if she were alive and free she would be somewhere in that station now. She had to be! There was only one train a day for Ostrowiec, and it was leaving soon.

We couldn't find her. She wasn't there. Benek and I exchanged a brief, worried glance. What should we do? We really had no choice. The train was coming, and we had to be on it. At least Rumka knew where we were going, we told ourselves. With luck, maybe she'd meet us in Ostrowiec.

Escape from the Ghetto

21

We never saw Rumka again. She never arrived in Ostrowiec, and she never returned to Piotrków. To this day no one knows what happened to her.

We boarded the train when it came in and found seats in separate compartments. From time to time we stole glimpses of each other, just to assure ourselves that all was well. But that was all. We didn't try to talk.

I sat by the window looking out as the train made its way across southeastern Poland. Broad fields stretched out to the horizon as far as I could see. A chilly autumn rain poured down in sheets. From time to time the train passed small towns—whistle stops, really—and there I saw Jews. All the Jews left in the little towns along the railroad. They were sitting in even rows along the tracks with two or three guards watching over them. Men, women holding babies, small children, all sitting with their bundles in the cold rain, waiting for the trains to take them away. These were the dreaded transports. I was seeing them for the first time, and my heart shriveled inside me. I saw shivering children, soaked to the skin by the rain, sitting in potato fields with their heads down, knowing all hope was gone. I pressed my face against the window. I had to see it all. I had to see as much as I could and more for the sake of each one of those miserable souls whose pain and despair I felt so deeply. My heart ached, but I didn't dare shed a tear. My face was a pitiless mask. It had to be, because I wasn't alone. I was riding in a compartment filled with people, and traveling in Poland is a social event. People don't just sit. They talk, and before long a lively conversation is going on among total strangers. And no matter where the conversation begins— gossip, politics, romance—sooner or later it comes around to everyone's favorite subject: Jews. They howled like jackals when we passed a station, pointing gleefully at the people waiting in the rain. They made jokes—horrid, disgusting jokes which I had to laugh at heartily and pretend I enjoyed. After all, every Pole hates Jews, and if he doesn't, perhaps that's a sign he's a Jew himself. So I hardened my face and howled with the rest. I was learning fast. They were watching me, those vultures, just waiting for me to make one slip. But I was on to them. I wasn't going to make any slips. I was out of the ghetto now, and no one would ever bring me back.

We rode all day and all night, arriving in Ostrowiec before dawn the next morning. Asking directions to Mayer's uncle's house, we learned to our annoyance that the station was not really in Ostrowiec at all, but several kilometers outside of town. We had a long walk ahead of us. Benek decided he was hungry and went to get a roll and a cup of coffee at the kiosk. He asked if I wanted anything, but I shook my head. I was eager to get started.

When he came back, we set out, Benek walking several paces ahead of me so that anyone watching us would think we were two strangers who happened to come in on the train together. As we rounded a bend in the road we saw a group of laborers approaching, carrying their picks and shovels. As soon as they noticed us, they cried, "Hey! Turn around! Don't go to the city! They're rounding up all you Jews! Go back while you can!"

How did they know? Did the strain of our journey show in our faces? Was it because we were too well dressed or because other Jews had come in from that same station, seeking shelter with their relatives in town? Regardless of the reason, they did know, and they were warning us that our supposed haven in Ostrowiec had become a death trap. We clearly had to go back, but where?

We returned to the station. In spite of our desperate circumstances, Benek was still hungry. I sent him off to get breakfast while I sat down to think of a plan. Our only chance was to go back to Warsaw the way we came. I knew the address of a woman there who was active in the Polish underground. Her name was Irena Adamowicz. Our youth group had contacted her several times in the past. Perhaps she would help us now, or at least put us in contact with someone who could. On our own, running from one town to the next, we had no chance at all.

Benek returned, bringing me a roll. I told him to find out when the next train left for Warsaw. He came back with bad news. There was only one train a day. It left at midnight, and the number of places aboard was restricted. First priority went to people with an official traveler's permit. Getting one was out of the question. The only way for us to get on board was to wait in line and hope there would be some places left.

I looked at my watch. It wasn't quite noon and already the line was starting to form. Benek took a place toward the front, while I found one five people behind him. We had hours to wait, but each second seemed like the tolling of a death knell. What would we do if someone got suspicious? Our only documents were our false papers. We had no ration books, no work cards, we knew nobody in the town. In fact, we knew nothing about the place at all. If someone asked "What are you doing in Ostrowiec?" we were lost. That was why I didn't want to eat or drink. I didn't want to sit down or go to the bathroom. I didn't want to talk to anyone. I wanted one thing and one thing only—to be on the train to Warsaw and gone!

At about three o'clock a gang of teenagers came swaggering through the station. "*Łobuzy!*" I thought when I saw them. Hoodlums. Of the whole Polish population, delinquents like these were absolutely the worst: thoroughly vicious and completely without pity. Finding a runaway Jew, taking everything he had, then turning him over to the police was a game for them—an amusing way to spend an afternoon. Down the line they came, pushing, making remarks, looking for trouble. When they came to me, they stopped. I stood staring straight ahead while the whole gang looked me over. I knew why I attracted their attention. I looked too good. My clothes were too stylish for this little town. "What's this *panienka* doing here?" I could imagine them wondering. "Maybe she's a Jew on the run?" They gathered around me, glaring, looking me over. One stuck his nose right in my face. My mouth was dry and my heart raced, but I knew that if I showed the slightest fear I was finished. So I glared right back, hoping my face wouldn't betray the tension I really felt. They muttered a few curses and moved on. Only then did I let out my breath. But as for Benek, the railway man in Piotrków was right. They didn't give him a second look.

By six-thirty the line waiting for the Warsaw train was very long. The pushing and shoving grew unbearable. Benek and I held our places at the head of the line, but we had to fight hard to keep them. At seven o'clock the ticket window opened. The crowd began to move. I saw Benek buy his ticket. One problem solved. But there were still five people to go before I got mine. As I stood in line waiting my turn, a man in a railway uniform came over. "I'd like a word with you," he said.

"What do you want?" I replied, still keeping my eye on the ticket window.

"Where are you going?"

"To Warsaw. Is it your business?"

"It might be. You think you're going to get a ticket?"

"Of course I'm going to get a ticket. I've been on this line since morning."

He sneered. "That doesn't mean a thing. If you really want a ticket, you better be able to pay for one."

I got the message. He suspected I was Jewish, desperate to leave town and willing to pay him a hefty bribe if he'd get a ticket to Warsaw for me. And if I wasn't so willing . . . well, he just might call a policeman. It was blackmail all right, but he wasn't a good blackmailer. He didn't have the ticket in his hand, and I wasn't going to fork over my money just to see him disappear. Furthermore, I didn't really have that much money, and what little I did have Benek and I were going to need when we got to Warsaw. Besides, I was far enough ahead in line to get a ticket without help from anyone.

I answered him with all the brass I could muster, "What do you mean? How do you know I'm able to pay? Did you count my money?" Since he wanted to conduct this conversation in whispers, I raised my voice loud enough for the whole station to hear. "I don't know what you're talking about! I don't have any money. All I have are fifty zlotys. And even if I had a million, why should I pay you anything? I'm going to get a ticket for sure. I'm one of the first on line!"

"Keep your voice down!" he hissed. "Don't you see I'm trying to do you a favor? You think you're so smart?

You won't get a ticket. If you expect to be on that train, you better be willing to pay."

That did it. "Listen here, you crook!" I started yelling. "I'm not from Ostrowiec; I'm from Piotrków. I have to get back home. If you're so hungry for a bribe, why don't you ask the people from Ostrowiec to pay?" I knew my rights. Out-of-town passengers had first priority in buying tickets on restricted trains.

The railway man rolled his eyes. This confrontation was more than he bargained for. He must have guessed wrong. Since when do Jews act like this? Instead of a meek, frightened girl, here was a loud-mouthed young woman calling him a crook in front of the whole station! He turned around and scurried out the door like a frightened cockroach while I laughed and thought of my father's words: "Never show fear to your enemies, because if they think you are afraid of them, they are absolutely merciless. Instead, attack your attacker. Always do the unexpected."

Once again he was right. For the second time I owed him my life.

"One way to Warsaw, please," I said, stepping up to the ticket window.

"You're not from Ostrowiec, are you?" the ticket man asked.

"No," I said, showing my passport. "Piotrków."

Sure enough, I got my ticket.

The Shop
in Rudniki

We arrived in Warsaw shortly before noon the next day and asked directions to Miss Adamowicz's address. It turned out to be in one of the city's most exclusive neighborhoods. The streets and houses were beautifully kept, but what impressed us most was not so much the elegant air as the serene quiet that hovered over the district. Coming as we did from the clattering tumult of the trains and the total chaos of the railway terminals, such stillness struck us as positively eerie, as if we had somehow wandered into a secret cul-de-sac where the turmoil of daily events was as inconsequential as an afternoon sun shower.

We located the address and went inside. We found

ourselves in a beautiful lobby decorated with ceramic tiles and bunches of oleanders arranged in ceramic pots. We looked up the name "Adamowicz" in the tenants' register. The apartment was on the second floor. As we walked up, I remembered a line from Hermann Hesse's novel *Steppenwolf*, a book I had read years before. Entering a house, Steppenwolf is struck by what he describes as its "middle-class smell." As Benek and I climbed those graceful stairs to Miss Adamowicz's apartment, I suddenly realized what Hesse meant. Like Steppenwolf, tormented, driven, terrified by his own surging emotions, I, too, marveled at the fate that had led me to this oddly tranquil place that seemed light-years away from the terror that lurked outside its doors.

We rang. The doorbell tinkled with a silvery chime. An old woman with aristocratic features answered. "Yes?" she said tentatively, standing in the doorway. "What can I do for you?"

"Is Miss Adamowicz in?" we asked. She invited us to come inside. We found ourselves in a beautifully furnished foyer that was as large as an average living room.

"What do you want with Miss Adamowicz?"

"It's about my brother," I replied. "He's having problems at home. I was hoping Miss Adamowicz would know what to do." Miss Adamowicz was a social worker who specialized in counseling delinquent boys. An active member of the Polish Resistance, she used her contacts with the Scouts and other youth organizations to deliver messages and food to the Warsaw ghetto. All our correspondence with the ghetto underground went through her. I had no idea how much the woman we were talking to knew about these activities, but I was determined not to reveal any more than I absolutely had to.

"Miss Adamowicz is gone, and she won't be back for a while," I was told. "She's visiting the orphanage. If you hurry, you might be able to catch her. I'll write the address down for you." As the woman went to get a pencil and a piece of paper, I asked if I might use the bathroom. "It's just down the hall," she said, pointing the way.

The bathroom, ten feet square, was a palace of gleaming white tile and marble. As I shut the door, I realized that nearly two days had passed since I last went to the toilet. With all my energy focused on staying alive, I hadn't paid any attention at all to my physical needs. I sat down with shuddering relief. When I finished, I turned on the faucet to wash my hands and a flood of deliciously hot water came gushing out. I splashed some on my face. It felt so good I decided I was not leaving that room until I had had a bath. Stripping off my clothes and using plenty of hot water, I scrubbed with Miss Adamowicz's fine perfumed soap and dried myself off with her luxurious towels.

I was nearly finished when the old woman began pounding on the door. "Is everything all right? What are you doing in there? Why are you taking so long?"

"One minute, please," I replied through the locked door. "I'll be out soon, as soon as I finish washing." I rinsed the last of the soap from my face. I felt wonderfully refreshed. Now I was ready to take on the world.

The old woman looked annoyed when I finally emerged from the bathroom. She handed me the address of the orphanage and showed us the door. I thanked her and left quickly, which suited us both. Then Benek and I set off to find Miss Adamowicz.

It took us a while to locate the orphanage, only to find we were too late. Miss Adamowicz had just gone back to her office. She was leaving town for several days on business, we were told, but if we hurried we might still be able to catch her. We hopped on a tram and after an agonizingly slow ride arrived in front of the old courthouse building. Miss Adamowicz's office was on the top floor. We tore up the rickety stairs and found a door marked "JUVENILE PROGRAMS—BOYS."

I knocked.

"Come in," a voice answered. Benek and I entered.

A man was sitting at one of two desks in the room. The other was empty. He asked if he could help us.

"We came to see Miss Adamowicz," I said.

"Miss Adamowicz is out of the office right now, but if you'd like to wait outside, I'm sure she'll be able to see you in a few minutes."

We went out and sat down on a bench. After what seemed like hours, the door opened and the same man told us to come in. Miss Adamowicz was waiting at her desk: a prim, slender woman in her mid-thirties with short brownish blonde hair. Her voice was very proper and businesslike.

"What can I do for you?"

"Oh, Miss Irena," I started to say, "our family is in terrible trouble." This was an underground code phrase meaning that the town we had just come from was *Judenrein*—"Jew-free," that is, all the Jews had been deported—and now we had nowhere to go. As soon as I said those terrible words, the seething emotions of the last two days came pouring out in great, heart-rending sobs. Miss Adamowicz sat me down in the chair next to her desk and gave me a handkerchief.

"Go ahead. Cry," she said. "Don't hold anything back. Let the tears flow."

It was a while before I was composed enough to continue. I explained that Benek and I had come to Warsaw without any idea of where to go or what to do. Could she help us? Miss Adamowicz wrote a telephone number down on a piece of paper and handed it to me. She didn't have to explain further. It was the secret number of the Jewish underground inside the ghetto. I was to call that number and get in touch with them. It was all the help she could give me.

We thanked her and left. Around the corner from the courthouse we found a small dairy store. Benek sat down and had a glass of milk and a roll while I went to dial the number. I heard the phone ringing at the other end, and then a voice.

"Yes?"

I suddenly realized I didn't know any of the passwords. All I had was the phone number. Then I remembered a young man in the Warsaw underground who used to come to our city to deliver illegal newspapers. We called him Wyga.

"Is Wyga there?" I asked. "Can I speak to Wyga? I just came from Piotrków, and the family is in big trouble."

There was a pause at the other end. Then another voice came on. "What's your name?"

"Ruszka Guterman."

"What are you wearing?"

"A gray coat with a sealskin collar. Oh, and a crocheted hat. It covers my ears."

"Good. Do you know the tram station on the Aleje Ujazdowskie?"

"Yes."

"Be there tomorrow at eleven o'clock. Someone will contact you." The line went dead.

I hung up the phone and joined Benek at the table. He

ordered another roll and two glasses of milk while I explained the situation. Now all we had to do was find a place to stay for the night. Hopefully the hotel situation in Warsaw was better than that in Piotrków.

It wasn't. Up and down the streets we walked, stopping at every hotel, asking if a room was available. The answer was always the same: "No." Finally we came to the Hotel Polski, the largest, most elegant hotel in Warsaw. While Benek waited outside, I went in and asked if there were any rooms. There was one: a double room with two beds. The price was astronomical and I really only wanted a single, but since I was having no luck anywhere else, I decided to take it. I registered, paid in advance, and left my suitcase in the room. Then I went back outside, met Benek, and started looking for a room for him.

We walked for hours. It began to get dark. It seemed there wasn't another room in all of Warsaw. We finally decided there was no point in looking further and went back to my hotel.

"This is my cousin," I explained to the desk clerk. "We've been walking all over the city, and we can't find a room for him. Since I have two beds in my room, will it be all right if he stays there with me tonight?"

The clerk sighed. "It's your room, Miss. You can do as you please. But you seem like a nice girl, so I'll be frank. The police raid these hotels all the time. If they find a man in your room—even if he really is your cousin—they'll give you a yellow book." When a girl was issued a yellow book, it meant she was officially registered as a prostitute—not the sort of thing I wanted on my record. But what were we to do? Benek couldn't spend the night in the street.

We decided to try again to find another room. This time we were lucky. Shortly before six we came upon a

The Shop in Rudniki

small, shabby hotel. "I'd like a room for my cousin," I said to the clerk.

"Sorry. There are no rooms available."

"Well, in that case do you have a spare closet? Could you take out the mops and brooms and let him sleep on the floor? Is there a chair where he could sit up for the night? We'll gladly pay whatever you want, but I must find a place for him. Curfew is at eight and the Germans will throw him in jail if they catch him out on the street. Please, I'm desperate! Can't you help me?"

He frowned. "Well, I did have a man who checked out this morning and wasn't sure if he'd be back. He asked me to hold a room for him until six. It's almost six now. If he's not back by then, I guess I can let your cousin have it."

We spent an agonizing few minutes in the lobby wondering if the man would show up. But six o'clock came without any sign of him, so the clerk gave my brother the room. That crisis solved, we went out to find something to eat. We found a small grocery store and bought radishes, salami, and bread. These we brought back to Benek's hotel. Then we sat down to our own little feast. How we cried, Benek and I, for sorrow and yet for joy. In spite of all the odds, all the dangers, we were still alive, still free, and still very much together.

The next day we waited by the tramway station on the Aleje Ujazdowskie, but no one met us. For an hour we walked back and forth, studying every stranger's face, hoping he or she might be the one to make contact—but nothing happened. Finally we gave up. I went back to the Hotel Polski and dialed the number Miss Adamowicz had given me. When someone answered, I explained again that I was from Piotrków, that the family was in big trouble, and that

I had made an appointment to meet someone on the Aleje Ujazdowskie but no one showed up. I was told to go back to the same place at the same time tomorrow. This time, they assured me, someone would be there. Someone was— a woman who played as much a part in the history of the Warsaw ghetto as Mordecai Anielewicz. Her name was Tosia Altman.

I was annoyed. Why hadn't anyone met me the day before? I was at the right place, and they knew what I was wearing. Tosia explained. It was because I mentioned Wyga. Wyga had been picked up by the Gestapo, the German secret police, and interrogated for several days. Then they let him go. Rumor had it that Wyga was now working for the police. Therefore, when I called and asked to speak to him, the group immediately suspected a trap. They checked their records to see if a Ruszka Guterman had indeed been one of the youth leaders in Piotrków and watched me the whole first day to see if I was who I said I was, if I was being followed, if I was with anyone else besides my brother. Only when they were satisfied that my story was genuine did they finally make contact.

We had a lot to talk about. Tosia suggested going back to my hotel but changed her mind when she found it was the Polski. Instead we went for a long walk. She gave me this advice:

"The first thing you both must do is find jobs. Once you have jobs, you can apply for working papers, rations, and residence permits. Get in touch with me again when you find work, and we'll take it from there."

So Benek and I bought a newspaper and began going through the want ads. I barely turned the first page when I found a job for him. In a small town on the outskirts of Warsaw a man was looking for a well-mannered, clean-cut

The Shop in Rudniki

35

boy (nonsmoker preferred) to be a barber's apprentice. Room, board, and clothing were provided in addition to a small monthly stipend. I knew we wouldn't find anything better.

"Well, Benek," I said, "once upon a time your name was Benek Guterman, and you were supposed to go to the gymnasium [secondary school]. But now your name is Tadeusz Stempien, and you're going to learn to cut hair." And that was exactly what happened. He applied for the job, was accepted, and went off the next day with 450 zlotys and his sister's blessing to learn the barbering trade.

Soon afterward I found a position for myself. A couple who made leather uppers for shoes was advertising for a sewing-machine operator willing to help out with household chores. This was a perfect job for me. My father's business was manufacturing shoe uppers, and I knew how to operate a sewing machine. As for household chores, how hard could that be? I jotted down the address and went over the next day.

A short, heavy-set woman interviewed me. She explained that the shoe business was booming. Her husband had just opened another shop in Rudniki, a small town about an hour's train ride from Warsaw. Their daughter had gone to assist him while she remained in town to run the original store. What they needed was a jack-of-all-trades willing to help out in the new place by cleaning, cooking, and washing clothes, and able to pitch in with some of the leatherwork. The woman said she'd like to give me the job, but before making a final decision, she wanted me to spend a few days with her and do the laundry. That would prove if I was a good worker or not.

I never saw so much laundry! There were at least three months' worth of sheets, comforters, and pillowcases in that enormous pile. They all had to be scrubbed until they were fresh and white. And what did I know about laundry? When did I ever wash clothes? My mother hired a washerwoman for that. We also had a wringer, a special machine imported from America to do the hard work of wringing everything out. Now, never having done a wash in my life, I was about to learn how.

The leather shop and the apartment where I was staying were on the ground floor. The tap, however, was upstairs. To fill the washtub I had to climb up to the second floor and carry the water down. Then I had to scrub and scrub the clothes with a big cake of lye soap, empty out the washtub, carry down water for the rinse, then repeat the whole process a second time. The woman kept coming back to check my work, and if the clothes weren't clean enough to suit her, I had to "put more elbow grease into it" and scrub them all over again. At last she was satisfied! But I still wasn't done. Now I had to fill the pots on the stove, heat the water to boiling, and set the laundry to cook. Finally, I had to wring it out, rinse it one more time, then wring it out again before hauling it up two flights of stairs to the attic, where at last I hung it up to dry.

I thought I'd never see the end of that awful day! The washboard scraped my knuckles raw. Each finger had a blister. Every bone in my body ached from lugging oceans of water down endless flights of stairs. I cried enough tears to fill a washtub.

But at last I was finished. The laundry was done. I had proven myself a good worker. I got the job. I stayed another three days helping with the shopping and various chores, but nothing—thank God!—was as formidable as that laundry.

The woman treated me nicely. She was very intelligent,

extremely shrewd, and likable in many ways. But, like most Polish people, she was also a bitter anti-Semite.

"You know, Wanda," she said one day while I was washing the dishes, "they built that ghetto to lock up the Jews, but I swear they're still all over the place. Why just the other day I advertised for a master cutter, someone to cut the patterns out of the leather. Well, a boy showed up. I tried him out, and he was very good. I would have hired him, but, you know, he was a Jew. I don't want their kind around here. I told him to his face, 'Hey, what are you up to, Jew boy? I didn't advertise for Jews!' " If I could fool her, I thought, I could fool anyone.

Then, on my last day, Benek came to see me. He had a day off and knew where I was working. I was out shopping when he arrived. When I came back, the first thing the woman said to me was, "Wanda, there's a fellow here waiting for you. You know, it's a Jew. What are you doing with a Jew?"

I shrugged. "It's only a boy I met on the train. He asked where I was staying, so I gave him this address. How was I to know he was Jewish? I . . . I didn't look in his pants!" That was good enough for her. I was learning fast. To pass as a Polish girl I had to talk like one: quick and vulgar, saying things that two weeks ago would have made me blush.

I was glad to see Benek again. He was doing fine. His boss liked him a lot, and he was learning fast. I was confident he'd be all right on his own. Before we said good-bye I made him promise to stay in contact, to let me know if he ever got in trouble, and not to take foolish chances. He seemed so young to be on his own, yet I knew his chances were better that way than if we tried to stay together. So were mine.

In the Mouth of the Wolf

38

I took the train to Rudniki the next day. Everything about the shop was bigger than I expected. The boss and three male assistants worked in a vast room filled with leather and machines. The kitchen was the size of a living room, and the boss himself was a giant.

He was about my father's age and twice his size, standing well over six feet tall and weighing over two hundred fifty pounds. He had been a sailor in his youth and had traveled all over the world. Tattoos of ships, anchors, and mermaids covered his enormous arms. He was bald, and, like his wife in Warsaw, he had shrewd, sharp eyes. He might have been rough and crude, but he was no fool.

His daughter was an angel. Her name was Krysia. She was just sixteen, with a lovely face and a sweet, gentle nature. My first job was helping her with the chores. We got up early in the morning, lit the fire in the stove, cooked breakfast for the boss and his men, made the beds, swept the workroom, and once a week did the wash, which was much easier with Krysia helping me. After the housework was done, we assisted the men at the machines. The boss assigned one of his apprentices to show me how to make the uppers. Before long I'd be doing it myself. The pay was room and board, and fifty zlotys a week—a good arrangement. I was prepared for a long stay.

My first jolt came one day at breakfast when I overheard the boss bragging about a new supply of leather he'd picked up "cheaper than dirt." I learned what he meant when I finished the morning chores and went in the workroom. The men were busy making high leather boots, the sort worn by farmers and horsemen. They were cutting the linings for those boots out of Torahs. I was stunned. Where had the Torahs come from? The boss found them lying in

The Shop in Rudniki

39

heaps outside the synagogue the day after Rudniki became "Jew-free." He didn't like Jews, but he knew good leather when he saw it. Since no one else wanted the Torahs, he carried the whole pile home. Now he ripped the end off one of the parchment scrolls and stretched it out between his rough, meaty fists.

"Hey, boys! Guess what this stuff is! It used to belong to the Jews. These are their holy books. So their God was going to save them, eh? Wow! Is this stuff strong! It'll make good linings for the boots!" But then he had another thought. "How dumb I am! I better save a couple. Then, when the Jews come back, they'll pay me millions!" He threw back his great bald head and roared.

I sat by my sewing machine dry-eyed as the men first traced the outline of the patterns over God's words, then cut the scrolls apart with their knives. I felt as if they were cutting my own flesh. And as the others went on and on about Jews, kikes, yids, I took those holy fragments, pounded them with a hammer, smeared them with glue, sewed them into boot linings, and pretended that none of it—the vicious jokes, the cynical remarks, the Torahs being cut to pieces—bothered me in any way. It was hard wearing that mask. So very hard.

At the end of my third week, the boss took me aside. My probationary period was over. I had done very well. He wanted to keep me on and even give me a raise, but as a permanent employee I had to be officially registered as a resident of the building. Mr. Kaminski, the landlord, was very strict about that. No one could stay longer than three weeks without being officially registered. He didn't want trouble with the police.

I told the boss I'd be glad to cooperate, but I would

In the Mouth of the Wolf

need a few days off to go back to Piotrków to sign myself out of my previous address. He told me to take whatever time I needed. I left that afternoon.

As soon as I arrived in town I immediately went to Mrs. Banasz's house. The minute she opened the door I could tell she was less than delighted to see me. The penalty for harboring a Jew was death, and Mrs. Banasz was no martyr. However, she didn't tell me to leave, so I made myself at home.

What an eerie feeling I experienced as I walked into that apartment! Nearly all the furniture was ours. The only pieces that belonged to Mrs. Banasz were the beds. The rest—the big wardrobe, the night tables, the crystal—all came from my parents' house. On the one hand it was like being home again, yet on the other it was very strange. Someone else was living in our home.

We talked. The woman's voice trembled as she described how she watched the Jews being driven to the trains. I asked about my father. No, she hadn't seen him. She thought she saw my mother and little sister, but again she wasn't sure. She was certain about her husband. She had seen him, shuffling to the boxcars—head down, shoulders slumped, totally without hope—before losing sight of him in the crowd.

"I made a big mistake," she kept repeating over and over. "I never should have let him go into the ghetto. I never should have let him get on that train. We should have moved to another city. I could have hidden him. I could have hidden your little sister, too." It was too late for regrets, but in a way I felt sorry for her. She was a broken woman. Her husband was gone. She had no children. Her only relatives were two brothers who despised her for marrying a Jew. All that remained of her life was a small apartment filled with the belongings of vanished Jews which she sold in the marketplace for money to live on.

That night I was startled out of a fitful sleep by the rattle of machine guns. It came from the direction of the ghetto in regular bursts that continued for hours. "Who are they shooting at?" I wondered. "There's no one left!" Then I thought of Mayer, my father, and so many of my friends. Were those guns aimed at them? While I lay in this bed, was someone I loved dying, riddled with bullets in a rubble-strewn alley or street? I closed my eyes and tried to block out those awful thoughts, but I couldn't. The shooting went on all night.

The next morning I knew what I had to do. Somehow I had to get into the small ghetto, to see what had happened, who remained. I asked Mrs. Banasz if she knew a way to get in. The most she could tell me was that at six o'clock two German soldiers marched the workers from the glass factory down Kaliska Street to the ghetto gate. This was a very different ghetto from the one I left behind. It was completely surrounded by barbed wire. German soldiers and Jewish police patrolled the only two entrances. Mrs. Banasz doubted anyone could get in. I decided to see for myself.

It was a quiet evening. Few people were on the street. Then from several blocks away I heard the clack-clack-clack of wooden shoes striking the cobblestones. "Their shoes are wearing out," I thought as the initially faint sound drew closer. "Many must be wearing wooden shoes by now."

I stood on the corner as they trudged by, the last Jews in Piotrków. They marched six abreast, heads down, clutching little bundles to their chests as they dragged themselves along, shuffling down the empty street like wandering ghosts returning to the graveyard.

Suddenly I recognized a face in the middle of that gray, blank stream. It was Shimon, one of the boys in our group. I once had a crush on him. He wrote beautiful poetry.

"Shimon!" I exclaimed as he came by.

He looked up at me with the great, hollow eyes of a dead man. "What are you doing here?" he said in a cold, expressionless voice. "Get away. There are people who will turn you in if they see you. Get away."

I ignored the warning. "I have to know who is left," I said.

"Mayer is left. And your father. Now go away."

But I didn't want to leave. "Do you need any food? I'll come back tomorrow. Can I bring you anything?"

"I don't need a thing. Don't you see the guard is looking? Go away."

I couldn't. I wanted to leap into that column, to embrace each and every soul, to share their suffering and pain. But Shimon would not even talk to me. "Go away," he kept saying. "Go away."

I followed them down Kaliska Street to the ghetto gate and watched until the last person disappeared inside. The next day I returned to Rudniki.

Now that I was a legal resident and had the papers to prove it, I began to breathe a little easier. The Jew baiting continued, but other than that I was starting to feel at home.

One Thursday night Krysia asked if she could borrow my belt. She was going to Warsaw in the morning to spend the day with her mother. She was very excited about her trip to the city and wanted to look her best. Of course I agreed. She promised to return by Saturday morning so we could get an early start on the housework.

I slept alone the next night in the alcove the two of us shared. It was long after midnight. I was fast asleep when I suddenly felt someone push me. I awoke with a start. There was the boss, drunk, sitting on the bed, grinning.

"What's going on?" I said. "What do you want?"

"No one's here," he answered, slurring his words. "Why don't you move over? We could have a good time."

I bolted out of bed at once. "How can you even think of doing something like that?" I cried. "You're old enough to be my father. Aren't you ashamed? Leave me alone or I swear I'll tell Krysia everything. How would you like that? What do you need me for? There are hundreds of women who'd come running after you gladly. What do you want with me?"

I pleaded, cajoled, threatened for all I was worth. He was a huge, powerful man, and if he decided to grab me, I wouldn't have been able to fight him off. Nothing seemed to work until I said, "What if someone did that to your daughter? How would you feel then?" That touched him. He thought the world of Krysia, and the idea of someone molesting her was enough to bring him back to his senses. He got up and went back to his own bed, grumbling. I didn't shut my eyes for the rest of the night. He didn't bother me again that night, but somehow I knew this wasn't the end of the matter.

Krysia came back the next morning, and we set to work cleaning the whole house. It was late in the evening by the time we finished. Only one chore remained: washing the floor. We were on our knees scrubbing down the workroom

In the Mouth of the Wolf

when the door opened and in came the boss and Mr. Kaminski. They were both very drunk. Grabbing two nearby stools, they flopped themselves down.

"Hey, Wanda," said Mr. Kaminski. "Come to the tavern with me. I'll buy you a drink."

"No, thanks," I replied. "I don't drink, and I don't want to go to the tavern."

"Aw, come on! We'll have a good time. Your boss was telling all the boys what a nice-looking girl he had working for him. I just want to give them a look at you."

"Now listen here, Mr. Kaminski," I said very firmly. "I am not going to the tavern with you. I have a boyfriend in Piotrków, and if I wanted to go to a tavern, I'd go with him. Besides, you're married. If you need someone to go with, take your wife."

He gave me a dirty look. I ignored him and turned my attention back to the floor. I heard him mutter something to the boss. Then all of a sudden he began speaking in a weird singsong. It didn't make sense, and it certainly sounded silly. He must really be drunk, I thought. Krysia began to giggle. "Mr. Kaminski, what are you doing? What are you saying?"

His arm shot out. His finger pointed at me. "Ask Wanda! She'll know . . . because that's *Jewish!*"

I froze, but just for a moment. "Keep your head," I told myself. "You'll be all right if you keep your head." He was probably so drunk he didn't know what he was saying. "I should know?" I shrugged nonchalantly. "Why should I?"

"Why? Because your name isn't Wanda. Your name's Sarah!" All Jewish girls were named Sarah as far as Poles were concerned.

"What are you talking about?" I answered, looking

him straight in the eye. "My name is Wanda Gajda, and you know it!"

"Oh, no, it's not!" he insisted.

Then Krysia jumped in. "You're crazy! Wanda is my best friend. She's not Jewish!" Everyone started arguing at once until Mr. Kaminski finally bellowed, "If you're not Jewish, prove it! Show me your passport!"

"Gladly!" I took out my passport and handed it to him. He examined it a moment, then slipped it into his pocket.

"This passport is mine now. I'm taking it to the police. I'm not hiding Jews in my house!"

He might be bluffing, but I knew one thing: I had to get that passport back.

"You don't know what you're talking about, Mr. Kaminski," I said. "If anyone's going to the police, it's me. Since when do you have the right to confiscate my passport? Who knows what you're planning to do with it? If you don't give my passport back right now, you'd better watch out!"

"That's what you say. Forget about your passport. I'm keeping it." He lurched to his feet. "Now I am going upstairs. Good night, everyone." And upstairs to his own apartment he went, taking my passport with him.

I lay awake that night making plans. I had to leave. There were too many "incidents": first the episode with the boss; now this. I had three weeks' salary tucked away in one of my belts for just such an emergency. But I couldn't leave without my passport. I had to get it back.

The next morning I went upstairs to have a talk with Mrs. Kaminski. She opened the door when I knocked, but I didn't go in. "I have something very serious to discuss with you," I began. "Last night your husband came in drunk and tried to get me to go to the tavern with him. I don't go out with married men, so I refused. But because I said no, he accused me of being a scabby, dirty Jew. Not only that, he took my passport away and refused to give it back to me. I need your help, Mrs. Kaminski, because if I don't get my passport, I'm going straight to the Gestapo. I can speak German and I intend to tell the Gestapo that your husband stole my passport so he could sell it to a Jew. I hope your husband speaks German, Mrs. Kaminski, because he's going to have to talk awfully fast when the Gestapo hauls him in. Believe me, I don't want to make trouble for you. All I want is my passport. Speak to your husband. Maybe you can talk some sense into him."

By the time I finished, the woman was trembling. "Please wait," she said. She went into the bedroom. I could hear Mr. Kaminski snoring through the open door. A few minutes later she returned with my passport.

"Thank you so much," I said as I took it from her. "I didn't want the police around here any more than you did. Isn't it nice that we women can settle these things quietly among ourselves?"

She didn't answer.

Now I was ready. I came downstairs just as Krysia and her father were leaving for church. They asked if I were going with them, as I usually did. I said I had something to take care of first; I'd be along in a while. As soon as they left, I packed my suitcase and started walking toward the railway station. Suddenly I saw the boss coming down the street. Fortunately he didn't see me. I ducked into a doorway and waited until he passed. Then I continued on to the station, bought a ticket for Warsaw, and caught the next train out. And that was the last I saw of the leather shop in Rudniki.

The Shop in Rudniki

47

The Man
in the
Railway Cap

I went to Tosia Altman's apartment as soon as I arrived in Warsaw only to find she didn't live there anymore. I still had a telephone number—the one Miss Adamowicz originally gave me—but I was reluctant to use it. The underground changed phone numbers frequently to throw off the police, and there was always the possibility of the line being tapped. I had a better idea. Every apartment house kept a registration book of its tenants. When people moved, they signed themselves out, writing the new address in the register. The registration book was always kept in the janitor's apartment. I went down there, and in exchange for two cigarettes the janitor let me look up Tosia's new address. I copied it down, took the tramway over, and found she didn't live there anymore either. In three weeks she had had three addresses. Well, what works once works twice. I went to see the janitor. This fellow didn't smoke, but he did drink. In exchange for a small bottle of vodka, he let me copy down the new address.

This time I was in luck. Tosia was still living there. I found her in the tenants' registry listed as a private tutor. I looked up the apartment number, went upstairs, and knocked on the door. A woman opened the door and asked what I wanted. I asked if Tosia were there and was told she was out giving private lessons but would probably be back in the early afternoon. I thanked the woman and went back outside, where I waited until two o'clock.

As I was going upstairs, a tall, thin, blonde girl came running downstairs past me. I didn't have to look twice to know she was also Jewish and on the run like myself, but I said nothing. I continued upstairs, knocked on the apartment door once more, and this time it was Tosia who answered. She was very surprised to see me.

"How did you find me here?" she asked.

I told her it was a simple matter of paying off the different janitors and looking her up in the registry. She was very upset.

"Then anyone can find me!"

"Sure," I replied, "if you know how to do it."

She then asked me what I wanted, and I told her I needed a place to stay. Staying with her was impossible because her apartment was a contact point for several different underground groups. I asked if a thin blonde girl just left the apartment, because I spotted her as Jewish. This horrified Tosia even more.

The Man in the Railway Cap

49

"How could you tell? She's so blonde and good looking. Her name is Astrid."

"I don't care what her name is," I replied. "I could spot her right away." I could see that Tosia was frightened. Ignoring her own fears, she told me not to worry. She assured me that we would find some place for me to stay, but first she had to take care of some business. She put on her coat, and together we went to another apartment, where an older Polish woman was living. On the way Tosia explained that the woman had once been married to a Jewish man and was one of the few Poles who were sympathetic to Jews. The underground supported her and paid her rent. In return she let them use her apartment as a way station. At the time I was there four young people, ranging in age from fifteen to nineteen, were staying with her. Tosia didn't bother to introduce me. In the underground the less people knew about each other, the better. She went directly to a tall mahogany wardrobe standing against the living-room wall. She knocked, then moved it aside. Behind the wardrobe was a low door leading to a hidden room. We went in. Here there was no furniture, only mattresses lying on the floor. Resting on these were six teenagers, boys and girls. In contrast to the four in the outer room, they had very Jewish features: large noses, curly hair, and dark, sad eyes. They were all pale and nervous. It was obvious they had been in that back room a long time. They were desperate. Where could they go? Their faces would give them away the minute they stepped outside. Their only hope was to stay out of sight until the underground arranged some way for them to join the partisans in the woods. But who knew when or if that chance would come?

Tosia spoke briefly with a few of them. Then we went back to the living room, where she conferred with one of the boys. After that we left the apartment and got on a tram. We took it to Grochów, a suburb of Warsaw. From there we walked to a small farm—or so it seemed from the outside. Inside was a nerve center for the entire Jewish underground in Poland. Each Zionist group had its own area. Couriers came and went with messages and news from all parts of the country. In the two days I was there, I met young men from as far away as Białystok and Vilna. Meanwhile Tosia and the other leaders tried to figure out what to do with me. Their first thought was to send me to Vilna. Tosia approached me and asked if I had the guts for a dangerous assignment. They needed someone to carry messages to the organization in the Vilna ghetto. I wouldn't have to go alone. A young man had just come down from Lithuania. He would go back with me if I decided I wanted to go.

I wasn't too enthusiastic. It was a long way to Vilna. Getting there would be hard. Getting back might be impossible. What if my brother needed me in the meantime? Yet in spite of those reasons I probably would have agreed if I could have gone alone. But I took one look at the fellow they wanted me to go with and I knew I wanted no part of that mission. To this day I can't understand how he got from Vilna to Warsaw without being picked up by the police. He was short, dark, and spoke Polish miserably. I didn't think he had a chance and I didn't want to go down with him, so I declined.

Well, then, if I didn't want to go to Vilna, what about Kraków? That was another matter. Kraków, the administrative capital of the General Government during the German occupation, was far away, but not as far away as Vilna. I could get back to Warsaw without too much trouble if I had to. I would also be on my own. I felt much better about that because if there was one person I knew I could rely on, it was myself. Tosia asked me if I was afraid. I shook my head. As a matter of fact, I told her, I was anxious to get started. She gave me the address of a girl who would help me get settled. I was to keep in touch with her. Eventually the underground would find something for me to do.

Within a few days I found myself heading for the railway station once more. By this time the Polish railway system was in complete chaos, and riding the trains was an adventure. Most of the passenger cars were reserved for Germans: military personnel, civilians, and *Volksdeutsche* (ethnic Germans). Poles had to scramble for what was left. Since there was a lot of smuggling, hordes of people were constantly traveling back and forth. Ticket sellers sold more tickets than there were seats so that by the time a train left the station, it was packed. People filled the corridors, the spaces between cars, the steps leading to cars. There were even people riding on the roof. My only chance of getting on the train at all was to get on at the very first stop on the outskirts of Warsaw. Of course, I wasn't the only one with this brilliant idea. Getting aboard would be a considerable challenge even there. But trying to board at the central station would be impossible.

I arrived hours before the train was scheduled to leave and bought a ticket for Kraków. A lot of people were also waiting so that by the time I finally got aboard, the train was packed. Now one of the survival skills I had learned by this time was to find someone to travel with, usually a young woman of about my age. People traveling alone stand out, and that was one thing I could not afford to do. Once I was aboard the train, I looked around and soon noticed a young Polish woman who was also trying to find a seat. We began talking. I found out she was going to Kraków, too. "What a coincidence! So am I!" I said. We decided to find a place together. We walked from the front of the train to the very end, checking every compartment, trying to find a place to sit. Nothing! Every seat was filled. People were already standing in the corridors. But it was a long ride to Kraków, and if we didn't get a seat now, we would probably never get one. So we kept looking.

By now we had reached the last compartment in the last car. We looked through the window, fully expecting to find it filled, and couldn't believe what we saw. There were only six men inside—there was plenty of room. Not daring to believe our luck, we tried the door. It was locked. We knocked on the window to get their attention.

"Couldn't you let us in, please?" we shouted. "We'd like to sit down."

One of the men looked up, smiled, and let us in. "You know, this compartment is reserved for railway workers," he told us. "But for two pretty girls I guess we can make an exception."

Luck was with us. There were two long benches facing each other on either side of the compartment. My companion found a seat on one. The man sitting next to the window on the opposite side moved over and let me sit beside him. It was very dark. There were no lights on the train as a precaution against air raids. The train pulled out, and as my eyes gradually grew accustomed to the darkness I happened to notice the man sitting across from me. He was wearing a railway official's uniform, his cap with a red badge on it pulled over his forehead to shade his eyes. He was asleep. I wouldn't have thought anything further about it, but just at that moment a beam of light from one of the signals along the tracks came through the window and lit

The Man in the Railway Cap

up his face. I was astonished. I knew him. He was my cousin!

How did he get that uniform? What was he doing here? It was a fair guess that he had false papers as I did. But how could I make contact with him without arousing the suspicion of everyone else in the compartment? Fortunately he was asleep. That gave me a few vital minutes to think. I turned to the man sitting next to him.

"Could you do me a favor?" I asked. "Exchange seats with me for a second. I think I know that guy."

We switched. Now that we were close enough to talk, I gave my cousin a nudge. He opened his eyes, but before he could say anything I said, "Hi! You remember me? Wanda Gajda?"

For a moment he just stared, not knowing what was happening. Then he caught on. He smiled, told me he was glad to see me, and asked what I was doing on the train. I told him I was headed for Kraków. He asked if I had a place to stay when I got there. I admitted I didn't, but I did have the address of someone to look up. He considered that, then suggested an alternative. He had been to Kraków several times. It was even harder to find a room there than in Warsaw. The city was full of Germans, and most of the hotels were off limits to Poles. The only beds available were in private apartments, and even those were hard to find. However, he did know of a woman who ran a small rooming house. She was sure to have a place for me. He suggested we go to Kraków together, and he would help me get set up. It sounded like a good idea to me, especially since it would give us a chance to talk. I agreed.

The rest of the train ride was uneventful. The train rode through the night and pulled into the Kraków station at seven o'clock in the morning. My cousin had a heavy beard and needed a shave badly. He asked me to wait for him in the station while he went to find a barber shop. When he came back, we would get some breakfast and then see about getting me settled.

The Kraków station is an enormous elevated cavern with a long flight of stairs leading down to the street. As my cousin went down to find a barber, I seated myself on one of the benches to wait. I didn't anticipate trouble, yet I was nervous. It was dangerous to loiter in a railway station. Regular and secret policemen were constantly watching the crowds, searching for anything even slightly suspicious. I hoped my cousin would hurry. Fifteen minutes went by. Half an hour. I was beginning to feel very uncomfortable, wondering if I should leave, when a man came over to my bench and sat down. I didn't dare give him more than a quick glance, but that was enough to tell me I was in trouble. I knew he was a policeman. He didn't have to wear a uniform. The Tyrolean hat with the little feather that he wore was a sure sign of the secret police. Now I had to be very careful. My heart was pounding and my stomach was twisting itself into knots, but I didn't dare let the slightest hint of anxiety show on my face. I couldn't leave the station because that would put him on my trail for sure. At the same time I couldn't let him study me too closely. I got up, walked a short distance to a kiosk, bought a newspaper, then came back, sat down, opened the paper, and pretended to read. Now I could keep an eye on him.

He was on to something, all right. Over the edge of my newspaper I could see his eyes studying my face, trying to make up his mind if my features were sufficiently Jewish. I turned the page, holding my breath. He got up. I watched him walk across the station and call over a *Selbstschutz*. These were auxiliary policemen recruited from

The Man in the Railway Cap

among the ethnic Germans who were assigned to guard trains, stations, and railway crossings. Their black uniforms and red swastika armbands distinguished them from the regular Polish police, who wore blue. I watched the policeman and the *Selbstschutz* conferring. It wasn't hard to guess that they were talking about me. I didn't dare move. I sat on the bench and continued reading the newspaper, pretending not to notice. After a while out of the corner of my eye I saw them coming over. Keep cool, I thought. No matter what happens, don't lose your head.

"What are you doing here?" It was the policeman, the one in the Tyrolean hat, who spoke.

"I'm waiting for the train. I'm going home." I said.

"And where is home?"

"Piotrków."

"Are you from Piotrków?"

"Yes."

"Show me your passport."

I took out my passport and handed it to him. He looked at it quickly, then handed it back. He turned around and called out, "Hey, come over here! We have a girl here who says she's from Piotrków."

Another *Selbstschutz* came over and joined in the questioning, though he seemed to take it much less seriously. He asked me the same questions, but in a much friendlier manner.

"Tell me, Miss, where are you going?"

"To Piotrków," I said again. "I'm waiting for my train."

"Do you live in Piotrków?"

"Yes."

"Really? Well, what do you know about that? We're neighbors."

"Are you from Piotrków, too?" I asked him.

"I sure am," he replied, grinning. What luck! Here was a possible ally. I had to get him on my side. So I asked him, "What church do you go to?" He mentioned the name of one. "Oh, well," I said, "then we're not really neighbors because I don't go to that church. I go to the one where Father Krzyczkowski is the priest." I didn't have to make anything up. Piotrków was a small enough town for everyone to know the different churches and priests.

The *Selbstschutz* nodded. He knew what church I was talking about. He looked at my passport and said, "Oh, you're a Gajda?"

"That's right," I said.

"What a coincidence. I know your family." I could sense that he was coming over to my side now.

"Really? Which Gajda do you know?"

"The clerk in the courthouse."

"That's right," I smiled. "She's my cousin. My family has the soda-water factory." He knew where that was, too. By now I had proven myself in his eyes. He turned to the policeman and the other *Selbstschutz* and said, "Listen, men, she's all right. I know her, and I know her cousin. Leave her alone." They walked away without saying anything, but he stayed behind to talk to me.

"You know," he said, "the next train out isn't the best one for you to take. You'll have to transfer, and there's a layover in Częstochowa for several hours. If you ask me, the one to take is the night train. It goes direct, and you won't have to waste your time transferring or sitting in a station." Then he whispered, "Why don't I look you up the next time I'm in Piotrków?"

"Sure!" I said, trying to sound enthusiastic. I gave him

my address and we made a date for the next week. With that he excused himself and went over to join the other two. I went back to my newspaper and pretended not to notice, but I could see him arguing my case vehemently with them.

It was time to leave, but I couldn't just walk out of the station. My exit had to look good. So I got up, walked over, excused myself for interrupting, then said to my new boyfriend, "Excuse me, but did I get it right? The train I'm supposed to take is . . ."

He repeated the number, told me what track it was leaving from, where I could buy the ticket, everything!

"Thanks a lot!" I said. "I'm looking forward to seeing you. Don't forget to look me up when you get into town." Only then did I leave the station.

I was going down the stairs, out to the street, when I met, coming up the stairs, my cousin, fresh from the barber. As we passed I looked him in the eye and shook my head slightly. He caught on immediately. We passed each other like total strangers, never stopping for a second glance.

I walked on for a while, turning every now and then to see if I was being followed. When I was certain I wasn't, I knelt down and pretended to buckle my shoe. I knew my cousin was watching from a distance. Sure enough, after a while he came over and I told him what had happened. He agreed that it was a very close call. Then we went to find a place for me to stay.

The Bunker

It was very cold when my cousin and I left the railway station. Our breath streamed out in great clouds. Our shoes crunched over patches of snow that lay underfoot. Together we walked to a rooming house where a woman rented individual beds to people who were only staying for a few days. My cousin often stayed there when he was in Kraków. He asked the woman if she had a place for me. She didn't have anything. We continued walking, and I decided to try to find the address Tosia Altman had given me in Warsaw—Number 6 Kurniki Street. I was to go there and ask for Lodzia.

We found the apartment without much difficulty. It

wasn't far from the railway station. Mrs. Mokryjowa, an attractive widow, owned it. I liked her as soon as I met her. My instincts told me that she was a decent person. She lived in the apartment with her two sons and made extra money by taking in borders. Lodzia, the person I was supposed to contact, was one of them. I asked if she were in and if I could speak to her, but Mrs. Mokryjowa said Lodzia was gone for the day and probably wouldn't be back until six o'clock. She suggested I leave a note, assuring me she would give it to Lodzia when she came in. Then, quite offhandedly, she asked if I had just come from Warsaw. I told her I had. She nodded, "Then there is nothing to worry about. Lodzia is already expecting you."

I thanked her for telling me that, though for the life of me I couldn't imagine how Lodzia knew I was coming or even who I was. Having written the note, we left. Kraków is a big, beautiful city with parks and gardens and interesting places to visit. I had never been there before, so my cousin took me in hand and showed me the sights. The rest of the day passed by very quickly, and before I knew it, it was nearly five o'clock. My cousin was anxious to take care of his own business. Even though we still hadn't found a place for me to stay, I was confident that Lodzia or Mrs. Mokryjowa would certainly help me find something. I said good-bye to my cousin and returned to Mrs. Mokryjowa's apartment, hoping Lodzia might be there. She wasn't. She was in and had gone out again. But she had read my note and, thinking I might be hungry, left me an apple and two pieces of bread.

"Did she say when she'd be back?" I asked Mrs. Mokryjowa.

"No, she didn't say. It might be an hour. Maybe more."

"Do you mind if I wait for her here?"

"Mind? Of course not, dear," she assured me. "Make yourself at home."

An hour went by, then two hours. No sign of Lodzia. Maybe she wouldn't be back that night at all. While I waited, Mrs. Mokryjowa finished her housework, pulled up a chair beside me, and began to work on her knitting.

Just sitting and watching the minutes pass was making me nervous, so I looked over to see what Mrs. Mokryjowa was doing. She was knitting a glove: a five-fingered glove, not a mitten. My interest perked up immediately. My mother taught me how to knit when I was a child, and I was very good at it. I was always at work on one project or another, usually socks or gloves for myself or my sister. Once I knitted an entire wine-red suit. It was easily the best thing I owned, and I looked terrific in it. I still had it with me in my suitcase. Knowing how to knit was an important skill during the war because socks, gloves, and sweaters were absolutely unobtainable in stores and cost a fortune on the black market.

That glove was giving Mrs. Mokryjowa a lot of trouble. Having made several pairs myself, I knew they could be a challenge. The fingers are the hardest part. Four needles hold the stitches while one does the knitting. There was a trick to it. I learned it from my mother. Since I was anxious to find some way of filling the time, I asked Mrs. Mokryjowa if I could see what she was doing. "Certainly," she said, and handed the glove and needles to me. I started working, and in hardly any time the glove was nearly finished.

"I'd love to be able to knit like you. You've no idea what a time I've had with that glove!" Mrs. Mokryjowa said. We began talking. She asked why I had come to Kraków and if I had any definite plans.

"Not really," was my reply, "other than finding a job."

Did I have a place to stay?

I admitted I didn't, telling her how my cousin and I had gone to the rooming house only to find there were no beds available.

"I'll tell you what," said Mrs. Mokryjowa. "I like you. I think we could really get along. If you think you'd like to live here, I'm sure we could work some arrangement out." She explained that Lodzia was going to move out in a few weeks and her bed would be available. In the meantime she had another one, but only on a temporary basis. It was a bed she rented to a drug salesman who did a lot of dealing on the black market. He only used it the few days each month he came to Kraków but he paid for the whole four weeks to be sure of having a place to stay whenever he was in the city. Since he wasn't due back for two weeks, Mrs. Mokryjowa told me, I could have his bed. Lodzia would have moved out by then, and I could take her place.

What a lucky break! I not only had a bed for the night, but a place to live as well. Nevertheless I didn't want to seem too eager. I told Mrs. Mokryjowa it sounded like a fine arrangement, but I wanted to talk to Lodzia first before making a commitment. Mrs. Mokryjowa understood and assured me there was no hurry. But why not put my valise away? I was surely going to spend the night there. It was late. The other boarders came in and started getting ready for bed. There were five beds in Mrs. Mokryjowa's living room. She slept in one. The salesman's was another—the one I was using temporarily. The third was empty the night I was there, but it was rented out, too. And, finally, there were Lodzia and another girl in the two beds that were left. In addition there was a cot in the corner of the kitchen where Mrs. Mokryjowa's two boys slept together. All told, there

In the Mouth of the Wolf

were seven people sleeping in a two-room apartment, and by the standards of the time, that wasn't particularly crowded. I was already in bed when Lodzia finally came in. I wasn't quite asleep, but I pretended to be. What I had to tell her had to be done privately, and privacy in that apartment was out of the question. I woke up early the next morning and lay in bed pretending to be asleep. I heard Lodzia and the other girl get up, dress, and leave for work. As soon as they were gone, I dressed myself quickly and followed them. Lodzia and the other girl were walking briskly down the street together. I assumed they worked at the same place because they continued on together for quite a way. Then the other girl went on ahead. I saw my moment. I came up to Lodzia and introduced myself, telling her Tosia Altman had sent me. She didn't want to be late for work, so we didn't talk long. We made a date to get together when she got off from work.

What Lodzia had to tell me when we finally did get together was very interesting. She thought I was Aryeh Wilner's sister, which was why she left the apple and the bread. Aryeh Wilner was one of the leaders of the Warsaw ghetto underground. His sister was living on the Aryan side under false papers, and he wanted to get her to Kraków, where it was easier for a Jew to pass. I hadn't realized that, but the longer I was in Kraków the more sense it made. The University of Kraków was one of the oldest seats of learning in Europe and gave a definite intellectual flavor to the city. It was also true that for some reason the Polish intelligentsia always seemed slightly Jewish. They looked a little different as well—darker, with larger noses. Finally, there weren't many Jews trying to pass in Kraków, which made it a lot easier to get by. In any case, when Lodzia heard that a girl from Warsaw had come by asking for her, she thought

Aryeh Wilner's sister had finally arrived. She even made arrangements with Mrs. Mokryjowa for a place for her to stay. But she didn't know a thing about some young woman named Ruszka Guterman passing under the name of Wanda Gajda.

I delivered all the information Tosia Altman had given me and began asking questions. What sort of jobs were available in Kraków? How could I get one?

Lodzia explained that the situation in Kraków was a little different from that in Warsaw. The German military and civilian government controlled everything. In order to live in the city I needed a residence permit. But since I couldn't apply for a residence permit unless I had a job, the first thing to do was find one. Once I had a job, Lodzia told me, I could apply for a temporary residence permit. That was good for three months. However, the real trick was to find a job working for the German Army. Then, just before the three months ran out, I could explain to my supervisor that I only had a temporary permit and could he give me a letter stating that I worked for the military and performed a necessary job? That way I could have my temporary permit automatically changed to a permanent one. The advantage of doing it this way instead of through normal channels was that I avoided possibly embarrassing questions about where I was from and what I was doing in Kraków. Getting a permanent residence permit was actually very easy once I knew how. But if Lodzia hadn't told me, I probably never would have figured it out for myself.

"But how do I get a job with the Germans?" I asked.

Very simple, she told me. Buy a newspaper, and read the ads. That was all the help she could give me. Beyond that, I was on my own. But I didn't mind. I had been on my own before and was confident that I could look out for myself.

I began reading want ads. I also let Mrs. Mokryjowa know that I was looking for work. Her sisters worked as cleaning women in a German office building. She suggested I talk to them, which I did. She was helpful in many other ways. Whenever she heard of a possible lead, she passed it on to me. She let me use her apartment as my local address even though I was still only there on a day-to-day basis. But the actual footwork of finding a job I still had to do myself. Day after day I made the rounds from one office to another, filling out application after application, leaving my address with the secretaries so I could be reached in case anything opened up. I got absolutely nowhere. I was beginning to feel very discouraged when one day, quite by accident, a woman in one of the offices felt sorry for me and gave me an important tip.

"You know you're going about it all wrong," she said, shaking her head. "There's no point in going from office to office. The individual offices don't do their own hiring. All military jobs are filled through the *Arbeitsamt*, the Central Labor Office. If you really want to get a job, go down there and fill out an application. Your name will go on the employment list, and when there's an opening they might send you over for an interview."

Thank goodness she told me that! I could have gone from office to office for months, filling out hundreds of applications and never knowing why I wasn't being hired.

I looked up the address of the Central Labor Office and went down right away to fill out an application. The typist at the registration desk who took care of the forms was a pleasant, dark-haired woman in her early forties. Since she wasn't busy, we began talking. She told me she was from Zakopane, a beautiful resort in the Tatra Mountains. I knew the region because I had been on a camping trip there one summer. We talked about the mountains and the beautiful scenery, and I guess the woman took a liking to me because before I left she assured me my name would get on the proper list. In fact, she promised to see to it herself. It might be several weeks, but I was sure to get a job eventually. She suggested I check back at the office every few days to see if there were any openings.

By this time I had applications everywhere. If there was any sort of manual labor available for a woman—janitress, laundress, hospital orderly—I applied for it. Now there was nothing for me to do but wait. I started thinking about going back to Piotrków for a short visit. It made sense. I was paying Mrs. Mokryjowa ten zlotys a night for a place to sleep and had to buy my own food as well. At that rate I would be out of money in a few weeks. In Piotrków I could stay with Mrs. Banasz for nothing and sell some of the things my father left with her to get more money. I would also learn what happened to my family.

That night I mentioned the idea to Mrs. Mokryjowa, telling her I was thinking of going back home for a few days, and would it be all right if I left my suitcase and most of my clothes with her? I made it clear I didn't mind at all if she wore any of my sweaters or dresses. Her face brightened up when I said that. We were almost the same size and, while she was a very attractive woman, my clothes were a lot nicer that hers. I knew she was dying to get her hands on my beautiful gray coat with the sealskin collar. She adored it. I once let her borrow it for a date. I knew she would probably have it on two minutes after I left the house. I didn't mind. She was doing me a favor. I knew she would take care of my things, and if any letters from the Central Labor Office came for me, she would keep them until I returned.

In truth I didn't plan to leave for at least a few more days, but the next night the drug salesman showed up, the man whose bed I was renting. Mrs. Mokryjowa apologized profusely—she really didn't expect him for another week. But now that he was here, I needed another place to sleep. She told me not to worry. The elderly couple who had the apartment in the basement had an empty bed I could rent for the night. I went downstairs, told them Mrs. Mokryjowa had sent me, and, sure enough, they let me stay. By this time I had made up my mind to leave the next morning. Mrs. Mokryjowa would take care of my things and my mail, and when I came back I hoped to have a job and a permanent place to stay. I packed an overnight bag and caught the next train for Piotrków.

It was early December 1942, a few weeks before Christmas, when I returned home. I went directly from the train station to Mrs. Banasz's apartment. This time, though she wouldn't say it to my face, I could tell from her expression and her conversation that she was far from glad to see me.

"I don't think you should stay here. It's very dangerous. I'm certain I'm being watched," she kept saying over and over.

I tried to reassure her by promising not to stay long. I asked if there were any way to get into the ghetto. I wanted to find my father. She knew of one way.

On the corner of the Rynek Trybunalski was the front office of a semiofficial business known as "the Shop." It dealt in men's and women's clothing, shoes, and furs. Well-to-do Germans and Poles who wanted the finest custom craftsmanship went there to arrange for fittings. The office workers and the highly skilled tailors, furriers, and cobblers were all Jews whom the Germans exempted from deportation simply because the enterprise was so lucrative—for the Germans. Mrs. Banasz advised me to go down to the Shop and pretend I was a young Polish woman who needed some alterations done. Once inside the store I would surely make the necessary contacts and find out what I needed to know.

I had no trouble finding the place. The doorman in front asked what I wanted. I told him I came to have a dress made. Since all the secretaries were busy, he asked me to wait a few minutes. The young woman at the desk was finishing up an order when he finally let me in.

"I'd like to see someone about having a dress made," I said to her.

She looked up and nearly toppled off her stool. She was one of my best friends—Renia Zaks. I nearly cried out when I saw her, too, but both of us knew better than to say a word or drop a single sign that we knew each other because there was another woman at the counter ahead of me.

"Just a moment, please," Renia said. She finished her business with the other woman and locked the door behind her when the other woman left. Then we threw ourselves into each other's arms, crying, hugging, kissing, so glad that we were both still alive.

"Ruszka! Ruszka!" she sobbed. "Where have you been? What have you gone through? I never thought I'd see you again."

I told Renia I never thought I'd see her again either. I related a few of my experiences on the other side of the ghetto walls, then came right to the point. "I have to see my family, Renia. Can you get me into the ghetto?"

"They're almost all gone, Ruszka," she told me, shaking her head sadly. "The Germans took your mother and your sister off to Treblinka with all the other Jews. Your father is the only one left. If you want, I'll try to arrange a meeting. But we have to be very, very careful. There are collaborators everywhere who wouldn't hesitate to turn you over to the secret police." She stopped a minute to think. "Come back in an hour," she said. "I'll see who's on duty." She didn't have to explain her thoughts. I already knew. The Shop, and all the other factories and businesses where the Germans forced Jews to work for them, closed at six. Then two soldiers, one in front and one behind, marched the workers to the main entrance of the ghetto. Once the column passed through the ghetto gate, the Jewish police took over. The Germans were very precise about who went in and out. If two hundred people went out in the morning, two hundred had to come back at night. Not one hundred ninety-nine, not two hundred one. They were constantly calling roll, counting heads. But, as always, there was a way around if a person knew what to do. Many Jewish policemen were the dregs of the ghetto, collaborators. But there were also a few decent ones among them who took the accursed job simply to keep themselves and their families alive. Smuggling someone into the ghetto was a matter of waiting until a good policeman was on duty and letting him know that someone was coming in. Then, when the policeman made his count, he simply skipped one. It was easy to get away with as long as the final count was only one more or one less because sometimes the policeman on duty included himself in the count and sometimes he didn't. Thus, if the Germans or the police chief asked about the discrepancy, he could always say, "Oh, I counted myself" or "I forgot to count myself."

As it happened, my cousin Leon was the policeman on

duty when the column went back that night. Renia got word to him that I was coming in. Everything was arranged by the time I came back to the Shop. Renia gave me a shawl and a Jewish armband to slip on. Everyone in the store was trustworthy, so we didn't have to worry about informers. She explained what I was trying to do. Her friends agreed to help me by letting me march in the middle of their group. When the column marched, I marched. My cousin looked the other way when we passed through the ghetto gate, and I got in without any trouble.

Renia took me to where she was living, two rooms on the upstairs floor of one of the empty apartment houses. Both rooms were filled with cots. Men and women, boys and girls were resting on them. A small coal stove in one corner served for cooking and heating, though there was little coal and even less food. Another door opened onto a garret, which was directly under the eaves of the roof and was packed with clothes, suitcases, and various personal belongings. Renia asked me to wait there while she went to contact my father. She refused to let me accompany her. It was too dangerous.

As I waited, I began talking with Renia's friends in the apartment. They were as eager to find out what was happening outside the ghetto as I was to find out what was happening inside. Many, I learned, had sets of various false papers; a few even possessed the coveted *Kennkarte*—an identity card issued by the German authorities. They wanted to know what their chances would be of surviving on the outside, and I, speaking from my vast experience of six weeks, shared what I knew. "It's very hard," I told them. "I don't even know if I want to go back. In the ghetto, no matter how hard conditions are, you are still with your family and friends. On the other side you are completely alone. There is no one to turn to, no one to share your thoughts or feelings with. The Poles are watching you all the time. The slightest slip, the least bit of bad luck, and you are lost." I don't know if I convinced them. Perhaps it is human nature to think things are better on the other side of the wall. At that point the conversation ended because Renia returned. My father was with her.

I could not believe what I saw. Standing before me was an old, old man, bent, gray, with a haggard, lined face. The last time I had seen my father his hair had been coal black. He was strong and fit. His posture was perfect, as befitted a former sergeant in the tsar's army. It was my father who taught me the leaps and kicks of those joyous Russian dances we both loved. It was he who taught me how to climb fences and trees. It was he who gave me the important advice about surviving as a fugitive—advice that saved my life more than once. Whatever courage and resourcefulness I had, he gave me. Was this the same man? He had aged thirty years in the past six weeks.

"Tata!" I cried, throwing myself into his arms. "Tata! What happened?"

"Later, later, Rushkaleh," he whispered. "Oh, my, you must be starving. Look. I brought you food." He had money, too, that he wanted to give me. He was worried that I might not have enough. I didn't want to take anything from him. I knew how desperate conditions were in the ghetto. I knew my father would give me his last penny, his last crust of bread, and pretend he had plenty more. This food and money might be all he had. I didn't want it. I didn't need it. All I wanted was the story.

"Tata," I said again. "What happened to Mama? What happened to Polcia?"

My father told me that when he saw the end of the

ghetto approaching, he and two of our neighbors, Mr. Israelevitch and Mr. Blaustein, began building a bunker. Benek and I were completely unaware of this because Father didn't want us to go into hiding with the rest of the family. He knew our chances were better on the other side. The idea actually began with Mr. Israelevitch, who lived upstairs. He began working on a hiding place on the far corner of the attic, on the side away from the street. It was a good location. A person had to crawl on his hands and knees to get into it. Anyone searching the attic could walk right by the entrance and never know it was there. The main problem was water. People can hide a long time without food, but they must have water for drinking and to flush away human wastes. Without some means of disposing of wastes, a closed-in room quickly becomes unbearable. Mr. Israelevitch had a good plan. He wanted to run a pipe from the apartment main into the attic, but it was too big a job for one man. He needed help, and the logical person to assist him was my father. As a soldier, my father had learned all about running pipes and building things. So had Mr. Israelevitch, who had been in the Army, too. However, to get the pipe into the attic, they had to run it through Mr. Blaustein's apartment. Mr. Blaustein was a tiny man who didn't know a thing about tools. He was no help at all, but he was included all the same simply because there was no way to keep the secret from him.

The bunker was designed and provisioned to accommodate twelve people: my parents, my little sister, and my aunt; Mr. Banasz; Mr. Israelevitch, his wife, and two daughters; and Mr. and Mrs. Blaustein and their daughter. How long did they plan to stay there? Certainly not forever, but long enough to buy time: time to gather their thoughts and resources; time to assess developments and possibilities; time to make new plans. Our apartment house lay outside the boundaries of the new ghetto being set up to house the "privileged" Jews exempt from deportation, but there might be a way of smuggling themselves in there. It might be possible to get out of Piotrków altogether. They would wait and see. The important thing was to avoid that first action. Everyone knew where those trains were going.

It was an excellent plan, but something went wrong. Though they tried to keep the bunker a secret, the news got out somehow. No one said a word, but on the day of the action when the three families were about to go into hiding, twenty-three desperate, terrified people showed up and demanded to be taken in. My father and Mr. Israelevitch protested. There wasn't enough room and not nearly enough food for all those people! The newcomers paid no attention. One—a notorious wheeler-dealer named Shaya—told my father bluntly, "Guterman, if I'm not in that bunker when the Germans come, then you won't be in it either!" He meant every word. Either they let him in or he went straight to the police.

There was no other choice. They had to let them in— all of them. A small, cramped space intended to hold twelve now had to hold thirty-five. There was no room to stand or sit. People lay on their sides on the floor, pressed together like sardines in a can. The most they could do to ease their aching muscles was kneel. Other than that, they lay on the floor, hour after hour: men, women, and children. They had to be absolutely silent because there was a good chance someone might be listening.

The Germans were very shrewd. They knew that the old ghetto was honeycombed with hiding places. Now that the first action was over, the real work of rooting out the Jews began. With a genius for meticulous planning, the

Germans divided the area into districts and subdistricts, detailing armed patrols to search every block, every house, every apartment, every closet, every attic, every cellar to find those Jews who might still be left. Room by room they went, pounding on the walls, kicking down the doors with boots and rifle butts, shouting, "*Alle Juden raus!* All Jews, out!" They lined up the ones they caught in the courtyards, later to march them to the trains. Sometimes they didn't bother with the trains. They machine-gunned the old and the sick where they lay. Sometimes they tossed them out the windows or threw them down the stairs before shooting them. They showed no mercy to infants or little children.

For three weeks those thirty-five people lay in that bunker while the terror went on around them. Thirty-five people, unable to bathe or even wash, breathing the same stale air; their sole toilet a bucket and a small urinal they dared flush only at night. Thirty-five people, their muscles aching for exercise, nerves frayed, children frightened and whimpering, not daring to make a sound for fear of giving away their secret to the soldiers below.

One night as they were lying in the bunker, they heard a knocking outside. Although it was extremely dangerous to admit their presence, my father and Mr. Israelevitch decided to take the chance. Without revealing the entrance to the bunker, they asked who was there and what he wanted. It was a messenger from another bunker located at the far end of the attic. The people there were out of water. They hadn't thought to arrange for a built-in supply and hoped to get by on what they could bring up from downstairs in buckets. But now their buckets were empty and they didn't dare go downstairs for fear of the Germans. Did my father's bunker have any water to spare?

My father and Mr. Israelevitch conferred. It was risky,

but they decided to help. They cut a small opening in the bunker wall so the messenger could come at night to fill his buckets. It was a decent gesture, but a mistake all the same. The attic dust was very thick and buckets of water are heavy. One night the messenger spilled some water—only a few drops, but enough to betray them all. The next day a detail of soldiers came to search the building. They went from cellar to attic looking for signs of habitation. Suddenly the officer noticed the damp spot in the dust. "There's a bunker up here!" he shouted. "Find it! Bring the Jews out!" The soldiers began pounding on the walls, yelling, *"Juden raus! Alle Juden raus!"* The people in the bunker panicked.

"Lie down! Lie down and keep still!" my father and Mr. Israelevitch pleaded with them. "They'll have to take the whole attic apart to find us. Keep quiet, and we still have a chance!"

It was no use. Three weeks of hell was more than those poor people could stand. The women and children began screaming, but the first to crack was Shaya.

"Here I am!" he screamed, breaking out through the bunker entrance. He threw himself down at the officer's feet and, pulling out a huge roll of currency, held it up to him crying, "Here it is! It's all yours! Only spare my life! Save me! Save me!"

The German was quick to take the money, but he had no intention of sparing anyone. Now that he knew where the bunker was, he ordered the people to come out one at a time with their hands up. They came stumbling out like cripples, their legs scarcely able to hold them. Mrs. Blaustein couldn't walk at all. Her husband and Mr. Israelevitch had to carry her. The soldiers brought them downstairs and lined them up in the courtyard. They were still there when the column came back from work. People who saw them said they looked like corpses.

When the officer was satisfied that the attic was empty, he marched the whole group to the Great Synagogue, which was being used as a collection point for stray Jews. Even as he marched, my father was thinking desperately about survival. Whom did he know with some influence? Could he get a work card or some other kind of exemption? What could he work out for my mother and sister? At all cost they had to avoid being put on the transports.

Several possibilities emerged. German officials, SS men, representatives from the *Judenrat*—the Jewish Council, whose members were appointed by the Germans and were charged with carrying out all orders affecting Jews—were constantly leaving and entering the synagogue, so it was still possible to make contacts and send messages in and out. Everyone in that place was feverishly trying to bribe, plead, or cajole his or her way out before the next train came. Mr. Israelevitch had some political connections and was able to save himself and his two daughters. One day an official came and took them away. His wife stayed behind.

As my father was racking his brain for some way to save our family from the transports, a man, Mr. Holsztain, came in accompanied by an SS officer. My father knew the man very well. Everyone did. He was a known collaborator with connections everywhere. He pointed to my father and said to the SS man, "Him! I want him!" My father was a skilled craftsman who knew how to set up and run a shoe factory. This was exactly the type of small industry the SS planned to start in the new ghetto. Mr. Holsztain was also probably aware that my father still had valuable stocks of leather hidden away. No, my father was too valuable to go to Treblinka just yet. Here was his ticket out, but he wouldn't take it.

"Do you really expect me to go and leave my family behind?" my father said. He turned to the officer and spoke to him in perfect German, "How can you ask a man to do such a thing? My wife and I have been married for twenty years. I cannot leave her and my child behind. If you will not spare them, then don't spare me. I ask for no favors. I have lived my life. Allow me to remain here with them."

It was no use. They wanted him, and they were determined to take him. My mother realized this was the end. She would never see my father again. He turned to say good-bye, and in that moment she slipped my little sister under his coat. It was a very long coat that came down to his ankles. With luck perhaps no one would notice.

Mr. Holsztain and the officer led my father away, my little sister walking between his legs. Suddenly the SS man saw what was going on. "Halt!" he shouted. He tore open my father's coat, pulled my sister out, and slapped her brutally across the face before throwing her back with the others. "Herman!" my mother cried. Then she fainted. My sister began to scream. My father tried to reach them but someone clubbed him over the head. Again and again he felt the truncheon battering his skull as he tried to get back to his family. Then he blacked out. When he came to, he was in a tiny room somewhere in the new ghetto with his head wrapped in bloody bandages. My mother and sister were gone.

We were both in tears as my father finished his story. "Tata," I begged him. "Tata, dear, don't give up. Stay here a little longer. Give me time, and I'll get you out. I know how it's done. I have connections with the underground. Remember how you used to tell me to hide in the wolf's mouth? You can hide there too, Tata. I know I can find a place for you. Just give me time."

He shook his head. "Rushkaleh," he sighed. "Rushkaleh, don't you see? I don't want to live anymore. What is left of my life? I don't want to be here. They wouldn't even let me die with my wife and little child. But I am thankful for one thing. I know that you escaped and are doing well. You must survive, Rushkaleh. You must survive to take care of Benek. Even more important than that, you must survive to tell our story. That is your job. It is the most important thing you can ever do. But as for me, my life is over."

"Tatusiu," I pleaded with him, "at least let me get you a good set of papers. You never know what may happen."

"I don't care what happens," he insisted. "And I don't want you doing a thing for me. I know this is hard for you to understand, but back in the synagogue, when I saw your mother's eyes before she fainted, when I heard your sister crying 'Daddy! Daddy! Don't let them take you away!' I knew there was nothing left to live for. I am a God-fearing man. I cannot take my own life. But at the same time I no longer want to live. No. I don't want to live anymore."

To hear such words from my father's lips, from the man who was my ideal of courage and determination, was shattering. My will to survive, which I thought could endure anything, crumbled. I no longer thought about returning to Kraków. My only wish was to remain in the ghetto with my father and my friends, sharing whatever time I had left with them.

But even giving up wasn't easy. How could I stay? The Germans kept careful records. Everyone had to have a registration number, a work card, identification papers, and a ration book. I was just as illegal inside as I was outside. What was I to do?

The first problem was finding a place to stay. My father's place was a nest of collaborators. He refused to allow me to come anywhere near it. Renia offered to let me stay with her, which was no small favor considering that she, her three cousins, and three men were sharing five beds in one small room. It was a considerable sacrifice to take in another person under those conditions, but no one complained. They generously accepted me as one of their group.

Days went by. Living in such close quarters, we all soon became good friends. We broke up the furniture in the abandoned apartments for firewood, and when everyone came back from work there was always a pot of hot soup heating up on the stove. Then, after dinner, we sat in front of the fire talking about all sorts of things: politics, philosophy, religion.

The day began at 4:00 A.M., when the workers lined up for roll call. By six, heads were counted, columns formed, and everyone marched off to work. Since I was an illegal, I couldn't leave the apartment. Every day from four in the morning until six at night I was alone. I didn't dare light a fire or make a sound, so when my friends went to work, I took a few featherbeds to the attic storeroom, wrapped myself up to keep warm, and sat there the whole day.

There were several windows in the room, which provided plenty of light. I sat for hours, alone with my thoughts, listening to the wind blowing through the deserted streets. The old building creaked and cracked. The very silence had a sound. There was never a silence so complete as the silence of that ghetto. It was the silence of the grave.

Stored in the attic were piles of boxes and papers, all the belongings of people taken away in the first action, people who were no longer alive. I began going through them, hoping to find something interesting to read, something to make the hours pass more quickly. I found all sorts of writing in those boxes. There were letters, poems, stories, whole philosophical treatises . . . and a diary. I opened it and began to read. I knew the girl who wrote it. A lovely girl. She was fourteen years old when she went to Treblinka. She wrote about the landlord's son, a thoroughly worthless young man a few years older than I: how he was constantly approaching her, flattering her, trying to get her to sleep with him. She refused, but he pursued her. In the last entry she wrote that he had spoken to her. In a little while, he said, all the Jews were going to die, and she would die with them without ever having known what physical love was like. She was going to meet him, she wrote, "because I don't want to die without experiencing as much of life as I can."

How I cried when I read that! I cried for her and my friends and all the people I knew who were taken away in the first action. I cried for my mother and my little sister. I cried for all the young, beautiful Jewish girls all over Poland whose lives ended before they could know much of life at all. Surrounded by boxes of papers, by fragments of lives blown away like autumn leaves, by the dead, heavy silence of the ghetto, I cried for myself.

Around this time a rumor began circulating that the Germans planned to accept six hundred illegals hiding in the ghetto as legal residents. If these people would simply come forward and present themselves, their names would be enrolled on a special list. They would receive working cards, ration books, residence papers, jobs, and places to live. It was quite an opportunity, but if I wanted to take advantage of it, I had to act quickly because there were a lot more than six hundred people in hiding. Renia assured me there was no problem. Her best friend Luisa was personal secretary to Warszawski, the head of the Jewish Council. She went to Luisa that day and asked her to put my name on the list. Luisa promised to do her best, but nothing happened. Renia went back day after day asking, "Is Ruszka on the list? Were you able to get her on the list?" Each time the answer was no. She hadn't been able to do it yet.

I began to get suspicious. All my instincts told me something was wrong. There was no reason for the delay. Luisa and Renia were practically sisters. I knew that people with far fewer connections than I were getting on, yet Luisa kept putting us off. I finally asked Renia if there was some problem. She couldn't think of any. She advised me to wait and see what happened.

I saw Mayer. He looked very bad. The glass factory where he worked was the worst hell hole in the city. The rations consisted of a cup of dirty hot water they called soup and a slice of bread that was more sawdust than anything else. The work was murderous, and the guards enforced a brutal discipline. A few weeks before, one of them caught Mayer in a minor infraction of the rules. He beat him over the back with a two-by-four. Mayer's back was still raw when I saw him, but he was lucky. The German might have turned his dog on him or shot him on the spot. I had to do something for Mayer. I made arrangements to buy a few ounces of ground horse meat on the black market. I planned to cook a special dinner for him the next night: *kotlety*—hamburgers—just the way he liked them. But my surprise never came off.

That night, just after Renia and I had gotten into bed, someone knocked on the door. Who could it be? It was long past curfew, and anyone out on the streets at that time was liable to be shot on sight. Renia opened the door. It was my father. An urgent look filled his face, and he was out of breath from dodging through alleys and abandoned buildings.

"Tata? What are you doing here?" I cried.

"Rushkaleh, listen. I don't have much time. I overheard something tonight. I overheard Holsztain say tomorrow they're going to line all those people up . . ."

"What are you talking about? What people?"

"The people on the list! The Germans are going to do something to them. They've got something planned. Holsztain didn't mean to say it. It just slipped out, and then he tried to take it back. But you can be sure he knows something about that list, and it isn't good." I knew better than to doubt my father. He had an excellent sense of danger. "Rushkaleh, aren't you on the list?" he continued. "Didn't you tell me you were going to get on? You'd better not be here when the Germans come, or they'll take you away with the rest. Believe me! I heard it from Holsztain."

My father pleaded with me to leave the ghetto at once. I couldn't decide what to do. I didn't want to go, but did I dare remain? As I wavered, a transformation swept over my father. No more was he the broken old man of the bunker. He was my father once again: tough, decisive, firmly in command.

"Don't argue with me! You're leaving tomorrow. You're not staying here for any reason. Tomorrow morning when the column leaves for work, you're going, too. Swear to me you will! I no longer care what happens to me, but you must survive. It is your duty to me. It is your duty to your mother. It is your duty to the Jewish people!"

Though everything inside me cried to stay, there was no way I could disobey him. I turned to Renia. "You heard what my father said. I leave in the morning."

That was what happened. When everyone left for work the next day, I went, too. The Jewish policeman on duty gave me a peculiar look when we passed his post, but Renia pulled my sleeve and we went by without any trouble. I went to the Shop with her group, where I gave back my armband, put on my lipstick and the rest of my disguise, tied a scarf around my head, and, at eight o'clock when the streets began to fill up, went back to Mrs. Banasz's apartment. I spent the night there and caught the train for Kraków in the morning.

Christmas Eve

I came back to Kraków looking forward to having a job and a permanent place to stay. I found neither. Lodzia had moved out, but Mrs. Mokryjowa was unable to give me her place because of the drug salesman. For some reason he took a violent dislike to me the one time we met and told Mrs. Mokryjowa that if I moved in, he was leaving. Mrs. Mokryjowa was very apologetic, but what could she do? He paid for his bed by the month, and when he wasn't there she could rent it for the night to someone else. She was making a lot of money off that salesman, which was why he was the one boarder she couldn't afford to lose. I understood her predicament and assured her I wasn't angry, but where was I to go now? Mrs. Mokryjowa said the old couple in the basement would take me in until I found a permanent place of my own. In the meantime I could go on using her apartment as my Kraków address. I then asked if any mail had come for me from the Central Labor Office. She shook her head. Nothing. Not even a postcard. So I still didn't have a job.

I went down to the Central Labor Office the next day to see what the problem was. The woman from Zakopane was at the front desk, and I was happy to see she still remembered me. I asked if any jobs had opened up since I was last there. She was about to say no, then hesitated. "There is something," she said. "A girl was supposed to be interviewed for a job this morning, but she never showed up. I can give that job to you." She filled out all the forms and gave me an address to report to the next day. I was now officially an employee of the German Army with the glorious title of "stairway janitress."

Early the next morning I reported to a military hospital downtown, a former Catholic school expropriated by the *Wehrmacht* (the German Regular Army). The building was four stories tall, and my job was to mop the stairs, all ten flights of them, including the landings! Believe it or not, there is a technique for mopping stairs. I learned it the first day on the job from the person I was replacing. You can't close off the whole staircase because people still have to get from floor to floor. Instead you block off one half of the staircase, sending the traffic over to the other side while you mop from top to bottom. Then, when the first side is dry, you do the other. And so it goes, from one landing to the next, from the top floor to the cellar. Of course, by the time you finish the cellar, the stairs at the top are dirty

Christmas Eve

again, so the job never ends. Many of the staircases had runners which I had to roll up and drag outside to beat out the dust. And I cleaned toilets.

After a few days on the job, I noticed that the only Germans in the hospital were the doctors, nurses, and clerks. All the patients were either Russians or Ukrainians. I asked about this and was told they were members of Vlasov's Army, a special detachment recruited from Soviet prisoners of war. I had little contact with those men at first since my job was to mop the stairs and clean the toilets. But within a few weeks a maid's job opened up on the third floor. Since I was a good worker, my supervisor recommended me for the position.

Being a maid was definitely better than being a janitress. There was more status, and the duties were a lot less strenuous. I had to make sure the floor was clean and assist the nurse when necessary. She brought the meal trays up from the kitchen, and I carried them to the men who were bedridden and couldn't come to get them themselves. Since I spoke Russian quite well, having learned it at home from my parents, I naturally began chatting with the soldiers when I brought them their food. They were delighted to find someone on the staff to whom they could talk. Word got around, and I soon became someone to them. When the nurse found out I could also speak German, she made me her personal assistant. I helped prepare special diets for various patients and kept records of who was to receive which menu. Whenever the doctors needed an interpreter, they called on me. On the one hand it was a good position to be in, but on the other it wasn't. The key to survival under false papers lies in making yourself as inconspicuous as possible. No one noticed me when I was mopping stairs. No one paid any attention to the girl who cleaned out the toilet. But as Wanda, the nurse's personal assistant, the girl who spoke Russian and German, I had a name and a face. That was not good. It could lead to trouble. But for now I was doing well. The nurse and I got along. She liked me so much she often brought me home-baked cookies and cakes as a way of thanking me for various favors. I didn't make much money, but I ate all my meals at the hospital and that was a big savings. Breakfast was a cup of coffee and a slice of bread. Dinner was usually a meat dish or else some nourishing soup. I often brought Mrs. Mokryjowa some soup bones from the kitchen. Although I wasn't living in her house, I still wanted to keep her as a friend. For now I was staying with the old couple in the basement. I had a job, a place to sleep, and free meals. What more could I ask for?

The old couple I was living with were an interesting pair. The woman was about sixty years old. I still remember the long black dress she always wore and her three strands of coral beads. She had been a spinster most of her life, working in a church rectory cooking for the priests. I never saw a more religious woman. Her husband used to laugh and say, "She's more a part of the church than the cross." It was true. She was always there. She went to Mass four times a day. And when she wasn't at Mass, she stalked around the little apartment, clutching her rosary beads, saying Hail Marys.

Her husband, on the other hand, was the exact opposite. He was an illiterate, jovial fellow who didn't take life too seriously. He had worked as a common laborer most of his life, mixing mortar for bricklayers, and only when he got too old to work did he begin looking around for a wife. The old woman had some money set aside; someone introduced them, and they got married. But there was no mistaking who was boss in that household—and it wasn't him!

On Christmas Eve the table was set for a fine dinner. The old woman was an excellent cook, and she had prepared her specialty, a prune compote, to crown the occasion. I had just come home from the hospital, very tired after a long day, and wanted nothing more than to go to bed. After all, other than keeping up with the necessary pretenses, Christmas meant nothing to me. The couple had just sat down to their meal when the old woman suddenly looked up, glared at me, and announced that she didn't want me around. No reason, she just didn't want me there while they were eating dinner. Furthermore, she didn't want me sleeping in their house that night. The old man was aghast. He tried to reason with her, pointing out that I was a nice, quiet girl who never made any trouble. I had already stayed there several weeks, paying them good money every night. I hadn't asked to share their dinner. Why was she getting upset? She had never made a fuss before. Why was she complaining now? The old woman turned on the old man. She didn't want me sitting there, she shouted. She didn't want me sleeping there. She wanted me out . . . now! So out I went.

Confused, angry, but not daring to protest, I put on my coat and hat and left the apartment. I considered my prospects. Where was I to go now? How could I possibly find another bed at this time of night, especially on Christmas Eve? I didn't dare even look for one. It was past eight o'clock and to be caught on the street after curfew with nowhere to go was a death sentence. Everyone in Poland had a home or a family to go to on Christmas. Who didn't have homes? Who didn't have families? Only Jews.

In the Mouth of the Wolf

Not knowing what else to do, I climbed up to the third floor, to the attic staircase, and waited. I sat by the attic door for what seemed like an hour, but when I looked at my watch the minute hand had hardly moved. Time passes slowly when a whole night lies ahead of you. It was a little after nine and very cold. I was freezing. The cold cut right through my coat as I shivered in the shadows, hugging the walls, praying that no one would find me and give me away.

Minutes passed like hours. Sitting, waiting, I lost track of time. Suddenly I heard footsteps trampling up the stairs. I pressed myself against the wall. But no one came. The echoing footsteps died down, and soon everything was quiet. But I now realized that my hiding place was a trap. The attic door was locked. There was no way to escape in an emergency. I had to move on. I waited quietly for several minutes, then carefully made my way down the stairs to the courtyard.

The courtyard was dark. Still, the spirit of Christmas permeated the frosty evening. As I looked up, I could see Christmas candles burning in every apartment window. There were the beautifully decorated crèches and Christmas trees adorning every home. In the distance I heard church bells ringing and the faint sound of choirs singing Christmas carols: "Peace on earth, good will toward men." But not for Jews, I thought. As I stood in that dark, empty courtyard, a hunted animal wondering where to hide, a heavy, wet snow began to fall. Soon my hat and coat were soaked, the damp cold penetrating to my very bones. Shivering in the darkness as church bells rang out all over the city, I thought about Christian love, Christian charity. I thought of Joseph, Mary, and the Infant Jesus. What if those three Jews had come into Kraków on the train that night, looking for shelter? Would all those Masses, bells, carols, trees, and candles do them any good? Hardly. The best they could hope for was to be thrown out into the snow like I was. More likely those holy hypocrites filling the churches would turn them over to the Germans. That night, all over Poland, there were Jews like me, desperately seeking shelter. But the inn was full. The well of human kindness was empty. Every door was slammed in our faces. And all the while, the church bells rang.

Then in one corner of the courtyard I noticed a large garbage bin set against the wall, but not flush against it. There was a yard's space in between—not much, but enough for me to hide. I opened the iron lid and leaned it against the wall. That would give me shelter from the snow. Also, if someone came downstairs to throw away some garbage, he could just throw it in the bin and go away. He'd be much less likely to see me than if he had to fumble with the lid. And so I crouched behind the garbage bin in the cold and the snow, slipping into the long numbing wait for dawn.

Hours passed. Although it was too dark for me to see my watch, I imagined it must be past midnight by now. One by one the lights in the apartment windows began to go out. I clenched my fingers and wiggled my toes to keep them from freezing while over and over again in my mind I thought about that old woman and what she had done. Did she suspect I was Jewish? What else did she have against me? Was there some way in which I offended her? How? What did I do that was so bad she wouldn't even let me sleep there? Then I thought of her little dog and how carefully she laid out his bed every night in the warm kitchen. How lovingly she arranged the rags in his little box so he would sleep comfortably. How carefully she prepared his food, making sure his little dish was always full. I sighed to myself. She cared if the dog had enough to eat and a warm place to sleep, but she threw me out in the middle of a freezing night with no concern whether I had any place to go. She had pity on her dog, but for me there was absolutely nothing!

The church bells ceased, and the last echoes of caroling died away. By now my hat and coat were so wet I could have wrung them out and filled a bucket. I tried, but I couldn't stop shivering. I wondered if I would catch pneumonia. There were still several hours to go. I stood up, shifting my weight from foot to foot to keep the circulation going in my legs. I squatted down and stood up quickly several times, hoping the exercise might help. I yawned. I was beginning to get drowsy, but I fought off sleep. Even so, against my will, I found myself leaning against the wall, closing my eyes. Perhaps I did doze off, or else I simply grew numb. Who could avoid it? The minutes passed so slowly.

Suddenly I heard footsteps. Someone was coming. I peeked around the corner of the bin. It was too dark to see much, but I heard a dog whining. It was the old woman's dog. The old man was probably walking him. That was his job. The little dog was whining and pulling on the leash, leading the old man straight to the garbage bin. He must have recognized my scent and known I was there. The old fellow looked behind the bin to see what was bothering the dog and noticed me.

"Jesus Christ!" he exclaimed, crossing himself in surprise. "What are you doing here? Why in the world are you outside on a night like this?"

"Where else could I go?" I asked. It was very late when they threw me out. How was I supposed to find another bed? The Germans would surely arrest me if they found me out on the street after curfew, so I hid behind the garbage bin to wait for morning.

"You poor child!" the old man sighed, shaking his head. He really was a decent sort. "I pleaded with my wife not to send you out, but you know how she is. Tonight was her big night, and she didn't want anyone else around. I tried my best to make her see reason, but you know I have nothing to say." He felt bad and wanted to make it up to me in some way. "I'll tell you what. She's already in bed. She just sent me out to walk the dog. When I go back. I'll shut the door, but I won't lock it. You wait another hour until everything gets quiet. Then come inside. Your cot's still in the kitchen by the dog's bed. She didn't put it away. You can sit up the night out of the snow, but don't fall asleep. My wife gets up at the crack of dawn. You have to be out of the house by then, before it gets light. And remember to wipe your feet. I'll catch hell if she finds out I let you in."

So that's what I did. I sat up on the cot in the kitchen for the last few hours before dawn, wet, exhausted, shivering, but at least out of the cold and snow. I didn't take off my coat. I barely moved. I kept awake by thinking of home—not the dreadful ghetto days, but the times before. I remembered the parties, the holidays, the summer outings to the woods and fields when my father taught me how to climb trees and jump over fences. I remembered my friends: our jokes and games; our long discussions; camping in the mountains; our future dreams. Where had it gone, my other life? Where were they now, all the people I knew and loved? Were they all gone? Was I the only one left? And what lay in store for me? Would this nightmare ever be over? Would this ghastly fugitive's life ever come to an end?

In the Mouth of the Wolf

It began to get light. I knew the old woman would be stirring soon. Very quietly I left the apartment and started off for work, resolving to look for a new place that day. I found one, too—a much better apartment on Ditla Street, much closer to where I worked.

I survived that night all right. I didn't get sick. But to this day I can't abide the sound of church bells.

Friends and Enemies

I continued working at the hospital, and, as I came to know those Russian soldiers better, they began taking me into their confidence. Few, I learned, were real Nazis. Most volunteered simply as a way of getting out of the prisoner-of-war camps, where hundreds of men were dying every day. They had no intention of spilling even a drop of their blood for Germany—not if they could help it! For them, being in the hospital was a paid vacation, one they naturally tried to prolong. What malingerers they were!

"I never take any medicine," one soldier admitted to me. I asked him how he got away with it since the nurse made everyone open his mouth to check if he swallowed his pills. "I hide the pills under my tongue," he laughed. "When her back is turned, I spit them out."

They complained of intestinal cramps, stomachaches, all sorts of internal pains—the sort of ailments that are impossible to verify. That was how they came to be on the third floor, where patients received a special diet of soft food.

Somehow they all seemed to have money. They often asked me to purchase small items for them: cheap tobacco, cigarette papers, newspapers, stationery. This was technically forbidden. But so long as there weren't any signs around, I could always say I didn't know the rules. It was touching to see how those Russians got along together. If one soldier had tobacco, he divided it into equal portions and shared it with his comrades, keeping no more than a single share for himself. They were a fine group of men.

As weeks passed, I became friendly with one soldier in particular. He was a slim, dark-haired fellow from Rostov. I often chatted with him when I was on the ward. He said he was an accountant. He was obviously a person of culture and education, and I enjoyed his company. We talked about literature—especially about Pushkin's poetry, which I adored—and politics. Like the rest of his comrades, he was eager to know what the attitude of the Polish populace was toward the Soviet Union, what the Germans were up to, and how the war was going. He introduced me to a friend of his, another young soldier from Rostov, very tall and also very intelligent. I asked if they had been friends for a long time, and they replied that they had been schoolmates together. Somehow I got the feeling that they shared a secret, and as I came to know them better, I was certain what it was.

Part of my job included stoking the coal stoves that heated each room. I started up the fires in the morning, making sure there was enough coal in the scuttles to keep the fires going through the day. The coal supply was stored in the cellar, and I developed such huge shoulders from hauling buckets of it up to the third floor that by the end of the winter my coat didn't fit. My friend, the accountant from Rostov, had one of those vague stomach complaints. Since he wasn't confined to bed, he often volunteered to help me with my chores. One morning as we were getting a fire started in one of the stoves, I decided to see if my sus- were correct. I waited until we were alone, then I under my breath in Russian, "*Ti Yevrei?* Are

He took a step back, paused, looked me up and down while thinking very hard, then finally said, "Hmmm . . . yes."

How did I know? It wasn't hard to guess. Not really. In fact, I suspected it the minute I saw him. His features and coloring were not at all Slavic. In fact, all he needed were earlocks and a skullcap to look like a perfect yeshiva boy. When he told me he was an accountant, I was sure. Business, mathematics—these are traditionally Jewish occupations.

"And you?" he asked me.

"I like Jewish people," I told him. "In fact, I have reason to suspect I may have Jewish blood. Don't worry. I won't betray you." I don't know if he suspected the truth about me, but after that we became closer friends than before. He told me all about his life before the war, about his family and fiancée, about his best friend, the other soldier, who was keeping his secret, too.

Once we began spending more time together, the other

soldiers stopped asking me for favors. I discovered that they had an unwritten law among themselves of never horning in on another one's contact. The taboo was even stronger in my case because the rumor got started that I was "taken." I was not at all happy to hear this because, unlike many of the other girls working at the hospital, I never sought to become romantically involved with anyone. Yet somehow all the other Russians came to the conclusion that the fellow from Rostov was my boyfriend. Whatever did they think was going on? He was sick, practically a prisoner, and I had so much work to do. Nevertheless, the more you try to deny a rumor like that, the more people believe it. I decided simply to ignore the whole business and let them all think whatever they liked.

A few weeks later my friend and most of his comrades were transferred and we were ordered to prepare for a new set of patients. Their arrival was a shock. Among them was a large number of Kalmucks, nomadic tribesmen from Siberia. They were completely uncivilized! Total savages! Not one knew how to use a toilet. Thank God I no longer had to clean the bathroom! Those brutes left the most disgusting mess everywhere.

My Russian friend wasn't gone too long before I began to miss him badly. I liked my job and got on well with my supervisors, but I was starved for intelligent company. I had little to do with the other girls working there. Most were crude, lower-class types, very jealous of the fact that I had risen to a maid's status so quickly. I usually avoided them as much as possible, but as the Christmas season approached, all sorts of parties and gatherings began taking place. It was impossible to keep to myself without arousing suspicion, yet taking part in those celebrations was a big risk. Whenever the staff got together at lunchtime, someone would start singing a Christmas carol and in no time at all everyone would join in. The gentile girls knew dozens of carols, but I knew only a few. I mouthed the words to the songs and hoped no one would notice. I began finding different ways of keeping busy during lunchtime. That helped, but some encounters were unavoidable. On one occasion one of the girls urged me to ask the soldiers to give us cigarettes as Christmas presents. I didn't like the idea at all.

"Why don't you do it yourself?" I said. "I'm really not interested."

"Oh, come on. We need you. You're the only one here who speaks Russian."

"No, thanks," I told her. "It sounds too much like begging."

She laughed. "Begging? Oh, Wanda, I can't believe you sometimes. You talk just like a Jew."

Once I made a very serious gaffe. A new girl was assigned to take over the cleaning chores on our floor to give me more time to assist the nurse. I explained her duties to her, and she said, "Fine. I'll look forward to starting next week."

"Great!" I said. "I'll see you Sunday." What had I done? Only a Jew would say that because the Jewish week begins on Sunday. For a moment I thought I was lost, but fortunately the girl wasn't too bright.

"Sunday?" she asked, very confused. "Don't you mean Monday?"

"Oh, yes, yes. Monday," I said, covering up very quickly. "Did I say Sunday? How silly of me. I'll see you Monday." I hurriedly changed the subject and got rid of her, but I couldn't help thinking how many other times I slipped without realizing it. I knew the girls were talking

In the Mouth of the Wolf

behind my back, and some, I was certain, suspected I was Jewish. There was no way to avoid it. My speech, my clothes, the way I carried myself, the fact that I spoke two languages were all evidence of an upper-class upbringing. What, then, was I doing working in an obviously lower-class job? I didn't fit in, and there was no way I ever could. I realized my days at the hospital were numbered and began seriously thinking of finding another job.

With the coming of cold weather, a booming black-market business in hospital supplies sprang up overnight, literally under the Germans' noses. The Russian patients sold blankets, sheets, and long underwear to the cleaning women, who sold them to people outside the hospital. Two girls on the second floor did a thriving trade in smuggled goods. They asked me to join them, but I wanted no part of it. Smuggling cigarette tobacco and writing paper into the hospital as a favor was one thing. Smuggling government property out was another. I had no intention of risking a jail sentence.

In the meantime groups of soldiers came and went. By now the population of the third floor was a mixture of Russians and Ukrainians and a great many of those horrible Kalmucks. One day a man arrived who was different from the others. He was a Georgian by birth but not a Soviet national. His parents had left Russia before the revolution, and he had grown up in Paris. The other patients were ex-prisoners of war and under close guard, but he had been serving in the German Army since 1940 and was allowed to come and go as he pleased. He was violently anti-Communist, spoke Russian fluently, and did not hesitate to express his opinions to the others. In appearance he was darker, more slender, and somewhat taller than the rest, but he was far from handsome. Deep pockmarks pitted his whole face . . . and what eyes! Huge, dark, staring orbs they were, ringed by enormous circles, as if he lay awake night after night tormented by horrible dreams. I loathed the man the first time I saw him. Just being near him made me feel sick. It had nothing to do with his face. Somehow I sensed a quality in him that was infinitely more cruel and revolting than even the overt crudeness of the Kalmucks. He disgusted and frightened me. I tried to stay as far away from him as I could, but, wouldn't you know, I caught his fancy. He decided he would make me his girl.

There was a small room next to the nurse's station where we kept thermometers and patients' files. It was here I brought the trays after the soldiers finished eating. Part of my job was to wash the dishes before sending them back to the kitchen. Since there was no sink, I carried the water from the bathroom in a basin. Every time I came down the corridor, there was the Georgian, waiting for me. I made it clear I couldn't stand him, but he paid no attention. He wasn't discouraged. He would not leave me alone.

"Hi, Wanda," he'd say as I came by with the basin. "Where are you going? What's your hurry? I only want to talk with you." I kept on walking, but he'd follow. "When do you get off work? We can go to the movies sometime. Tell you what, I'll even buy you dinner. I can meet you somewhere after you get off work . . ." On and on he went. Always the same lines. He gave me no peace. At first I ignored him, but that had no effect. He went right on bothering me. One day I lost my temper.

"You go to the devil! Just leave me alone! I don't know where you got the idea I'd ever go out with you, but you can forget it!"

It didn't bother him at all. He was after me constantly,

telling me how much money he had, how he was going to buy me clothes or treat me to dinner or take me to a show. If I disliked him before, I detested him now. He knew my schedule and followed me around. There he was every time I turned my head. He started making suggestive remarks. Every hour at work was torture. I considered asking for a transfer to another floor but realized that he'd only follow me there. What could I do? There was no way out. One day I decided to settle things once and for all, come what may.

I had a load of lunch dishes to wash. I went to the washroom and let the hot water run, then filled my basin almost up to the brim. I took a deep breath before stepping out into the corridor. I knew he would be waiting. I opened the door. Sure enough, there he was. "So tell me, Wanda, when are we going out . . ." I threw the whole steaming basin right in his face.

He howled! The other patients in the corridor roared. "Aha! We warned you!" they cried. "We told you to leave Wanda alone. You got just what you asked for!"

He was furious. "You wait," he snarled, glaring at me with those sinister black eyes. "I'll get you for this. You'll pay dearly."

"Ha! That's what you think!" I sneered, turning my back and sauntering away. But even as I put up a careless front, I knew I was in trouble. He was my enemy now, and somehow, sooner or later, he would find a way to get his revenge.

I didn't have to wait long. The next morning when I arrived at work, the doctor summoned me to his office. He looked at me very sternly, then said that he had received a report that I had purchased a hospital blanket and a pair of underwear from one of the patients. I knew quite well who the source of that accusation was. It was a serious charge, but fortunately the doctor liked me enough to at least hear me out.

"Sir, I have worked here for several months," I began. "You know the quality of the work I do and what sort of person I am. I swear to you that I never bought anything from a patient in this hospital."

What I said was the truth. But still the charge wasn't completely false. In these situations it is always best to tell the truth, and so I did. "A few days ago one of the kitchen workers asked me for a favor. She wanted to buy a blanket to make into a winter coat for her daughter. She told me she knew of a Russian who had a blanket to sell and wanted me to act as an interpreter. It was a simple favor, so I agreed. I even asked the fellow, 'Are you sure this is your blanket and not the hospital's?' He said it was his; his mother gave it to him when he joined the Army. It didn't really look like a hospital blanket, so I assumed he was telling the truth. I can't deny I was involved, but only as an interpreter. I myself never sold or bought anything that belonged to this hospital."

The doctor listened thoughtfully to my story. Then he asked, "Have you ever seen anyone buying or selling hospital property?"

Once more I told the truth. "I must admit that I have seen that on a few occasions. But I was never personally involved."

"All right," the doctor said. "But what I really want to know is how she got the blanket out of the building without being seen."

"That I honestly don't know," I replied. "Although after she bought the blanket, she did ask if I had an empty pail."

"And did you give her one?"

"Yes," I admitted. "I gave her my pail."

The doctor called in the soldier with the blanket, the kitchen woman, and the Georgian, too, because he had to sign the affidavit. The woman and I were put on probation. They allowed us to continue working, but we were ordered not to leave the city. Vast amounts of supplies were disappearing from hospital stores every day, and the authorities were determined to make an example of this case. There was going to be a full-scale police investigation. Just my luck!

Nothing happened for several days. Then, while I was at work, the police came to my apartment and searched through all my belongings to see if I had any Army property in my possession. Of course, they found nothing. This was followed by a summons to the offices of the Polish security police.

I arrived for my appointment at the police station at nine. The detective handling the case was a big, heavy-set man in his forties. He took me into a private office for questioning and immediately began making threats.

"I hope you said good-bye to your friends before coming here because you won't be seeing them for a while. We know all about your racket. We caught you red-handed. It'll be a long time before you see the outside of a jail cell."

"Really?" I replied with a sly grin. "That's too bad. But as long as you're going to throw me in a cell, could you throw a couple of good-looking guys in with me? Then I wouldn't mind so much."

Once I called his bluff, he laughed and relaxed considerably. "Okay, let's see your papers." He looked them over and asked why I didn't have a new identity card.

"I come from Piotrków, and we don't use identity

cards much there," I explained. "A work card and a passport are usually enough. I know I should have an identity card, but getting one means taking off a day from work and going down to city hall. Frankly, I can't afford to lose the pay."

"But how did you get by so long without an identity card? You have to show one to get rations."

"I don't need rations," I told him. "I get all my meals at the hospital."

The detective nodded. "I see. Well, that makes sense. But let me give you some advice. Go get yourself an identity card right away, even if you do have to take off a day from work. All civilians in Kraków are supposed to have them, and if the Germans catch you without one, they won't listen to excuses. Now tell me what happened at the hospital."

I told the same story I told the doctor but with a slight variation. I knew that as a Pole the detective probably hated Russians as much as he hated Germans. All Poles do. So I told him the story as one Pole to another.

"I work at the hospital. I do my job. I keep the floor clean, pass out the meal trays, and assist the nurse when she needs me. Nowhere does it say in my contract that I have to go out with those lousy Russians. I know the guy who made the complaint. You should see him! He has a face full of holes and these staring frog's eyes. No wonder he can't find a girl to go out with him! But just because I work on his floor doesn't give him the right to persecute me. I can't even tell you some of the filthy things he said. Besides, even if he were the handsomest guy on earth, I still wouldn't date him. I'm a respectable girl and a patriot. I'd rather die than go out with a Russian. Anyway, one day I got fed up. I was sick and tired of that animal annoying me, so I filled a basin with hot water and threw the whole thing in his face. He told me I'd be sorry, and that's when he went down to the doctor and denounced me. He tried to get me in trouble just because I wouldn't go out with him."

Then I started talking about the other woman. "What do you people want from her? She's a poor widow with two small children. The pay in that kitchen is next to nothing. Everything she earns goes to feed those two kids. I'm no informer, and I never wanted to get involved myself, but the truth is that everyone in that hospital is robbing the Germans blind. They take out mountains of stuff every day. All this poor woman wanted was one little blanket so that she could make a winter coat for her daughter. That's all. She asked me to talk to the soldier because I know Russian. So I spoke to him. I asked if the blanket was his property, and he said yes. Maybe I was naïve. Maybe I was stupid to get involved in the first place. But even so, no one can say I took money for it. No one! Now once the woman had her blanket, she asked me for an empty pail. Well, to tell the truth I had my suspicions why she wanted it, but I didn't ask. I gave her a pail and went about my business. What she did with it afterward I don't know."

But, of course, I did. She put the blanket in the pail, covered it up with waste paper and took it down to the cellar. After work she pinned the blanket around her waist, put her coat on over it, and walked right past the guards and out the door. No one would have caught her if that Georgian hadn't tried to get back at me. But in any case, the most anyone could say about my own involvement was that I should have used better judgment. That was the detective's conclusion when he finished questioning me.

The detective was satisfied with my testimony. I wasn't called to appear at the inquest. The nurses gave me an outstanding character reference, stating that I was honest, conscientious about my work, and went out of my way to be helpful. The doctor included these references as part of his testimony at the trial, and I believe they made a difference. The widow received a two-month jail term for stealing the blanket. I was merely fired, as the verdict said, "for being part of a conspiracy, though not deriving personal benefit from it."

Potatoes
for the SS

After losing my job at the hospital, it was back to the Central Labor Office to start again from the beginning. A different woman was at the desk this time. I asked her if she could get me another job like the one I had in the hospital. I told her I had been a janitress. She looked me over. "Do you know how to darn socks?" she asked.

"Of course!" I replied. "Who doesn't?"

"Fine! Then I have something for you. I'm sure you'd much rather have a sewing job instead of doing that heavy cleaning work. Besides, there aren't any cleaning jobs open right now." She gave me an uncertain look as she said that, as if she couldn't imagine why someone who spoke and dressed as I did wanted to be a cleaning woman in the first place.

"Then let it be sewing," I told her. It wasn't exactly the type of work I was looking for, but I knew that if I turned it down for no good reason, I'd never get another job through the Central Labor Office.

She gave me the address of a clothing factory in Kraków Płaszów that manufactured uniforms. I took the tram out, found the place, and went in. Five Polish teenagers—three girls and two boys—were in the front office packing tunics and trousers into boxes. I asked one of the girls where to go for my interview and was directed to one of the inner offices. I opened the door and found to my astonishment that the factory was an outpost of the small ghetto in Kraków, similar to the shop in Piotrków. The secretary at the desk, the foreman, the office manager, and all the other workers were Jewish. The only Poles were the teenagers out front. When I saw this, I knew I didn't dare take that job. No one can spot a Jew faster than another Jew.

I went up to the office manager's desk for my interview, but she immediately started yelling, "Who are you? What are you doing here? Who sent you in? Can't you see I'm busy? Go outside and wait till you're called!" Her arrogance surprised me. She treated the Poles in that place like dirt, constantly yelling and screaming at them. Later I realized why. Every job in that plant was a ticket to life for some Jewish man or woman. She didn't want Poles hogging those precious positions. In a sense the office manager and I were thinking along similar lines. We both didn't want me working there.

I went back outside, thinking all the while of what I

could do to make her reject me. As I was waiting, I started talking to one of the Polish girls.

"Hi. How are you doing?"

"Fine."

"Tell me something. The Central Labor Office sent me over to interview for a job here. Is this a good place to work? What kind of benefits do they give you? Any ration cards?"

She looked around to make sure no one was listening. "Hell! The Jews carry on here just like they did before. Better be careful you don't get stuck in this dump unless you want to be ruled by Jews!"

That I already knew. The question was how to get out of it without actually turning the job down. I was still thinking when the secretary called my name. I went back into the office and the first question the office manager asked me was "Can you sew?"

I saw my way out. "No," I said.

"What's this?" she exclaimed, getting very flustered. "Those idiots at the Central Labor Office! They know I need people who can sew! Why do they send me someone who can't?"

"Don't get excited," I said. "The lady asked if I knew how to darn socks. I told her yes, so she sent me over. How was I to know what you wanted?"

The office manager was furious. She took my application and scrawled "UNQUALIFIED!" across it. Problem solved. But I still needed a job.

At this time I was living in a third-floor apartment on Ditla Street. Living on the second floor was an older couple whom I got to know. These people had a tanner boarding with them who worked for the SS. I told my troubles to my neighbor, and she suggested I talk to the tanner. He might know a way of getting a job with the SS.

I went to talk with him that evening. He told me the SS had its own hiring agency, separate from the Central Labor Office. He gave me its address and urged me to go down the next day. "You're sure to find something," he assured me. "They're always looking for people to work."

Sure enough, I got a job. I was assigned to the kitchen of the Third SS Pioneer Training Battalion, headquartered on the Bernardinerstrasse, just across from the Wawel Palace. It was exactly what I was looking for. I qualified for a work card and got my meals free. But it was no vacation. The work was physically taxing, but far more exhausting was the mental strain.

I and five other women sat in one room from seven in the morning until five in the afternoon. We ate together, took our breaks together, and worked together for ten long hours. I couldn't have been more out of place if I suddenly found myself on another planet. I came from a traditional Jewish background and the class difference between us was enormous.

One was a prostitute. Another had been a prostitute but was married now. There was an illiterate Ukrainian woman working to support herself and her illegitimate baby, an old, beaten-down crone so starved her bones showed through her skin, and her fourteen-year-old daughter. The daughter was surprisingly pretty. Of all those hags, she was the only pleasant one. At least every word out of her mouth wasn't a swear word.

Our main job was peeling potatoes. We peeled mountains of them! Each women was responsible for her own. We lugged the potatoes in baskets, twenty to thirty pounds at a time, from the storeroom in the basement to the scrubbing room. There we washed them down, peeled them, and put them in big basins of water to keep them from turning black. We each had our own basin. When it was full, we took our potatoes to the sink to wash them several more times before dumping them into big steam kettles to cook. From time to time there were other chores as well: washing spinach, chopping rhubarb, hulling strawberries.

Spinach, rhubarb, and strawberries were a vacation compared to those potatoes. When one of us was assigned to an easier job, she guarded it like gold. Let someone try to horn in, and the curse words flew. It was the vilest, filthiest language I had ever heard. Even the soldiers in the hospital didn't talk like that. And when the women began bullying me and trying to push me out of the easier jobs, I had to fight back, cursing as they did, or they would have made my life hell. But no matter how hard I tried, no matter how often I mouthed those curses silently to myself, when the time came I simply could not bring myself to say them.

They found other ways to torment me. We would be sitting, peeling potatoes, and soon the two prostitutes would start telling the filthiest stories about their experiences. My face would turn purple with embarrassment to hear such things. Then they would howl with laughter, saying, "Look at Wanda! I bet she's still a virgin! Just like a Jewish girl!" As long as they teased me about being a virgin, I could ignore it. But when it started to be a "Jewish virgin," that was bad.

Once I went down to the basement to fetch potatoes. When I came back I caught the married woman behind the door with a soldier. I couldn't speak. I turned away, shaking with embarrassment and disgust. She really began giving it to me after that. "Look at her! She thinks she's better than us, our virgin. Our Jewish virgin!"

Our kitchen was responsible for preparing the recruits' mess. Every morning the soldiers lined up for a breakfast of coffee, a roll, and a pat of butter, cheese, jam, or salami. The big meal was served at two, and we spent most of the day preparing for it. Each of the various jobs had a definite status. Peeling potatoes was the lowest. The next step up was helping the cook, and it was a very big step.

I hadn't been working there long when I was promoted to cook's assistant. I chopped parsley, grated onions, beat eggs, and generally did whatever he told me to do. At mess call I stood behind the gravy or the potatoes and dished it out to the recruits as they came by. Since we also prepared the sergeants' mess, we sometimes got extra treats. The cook once gave me two oranges. I hadn't seen an orange since the war began!

What a character that cook was! He may have been an SS man, but he certainly had a sense of humor. When he first assigned me to help him, I was surprised because I hadn't been working there that long. I asked why he picked me over the others, and he said, "If I have to have hair in my soup, at least I want it to be clean hair." But sometimes he got fresh. Once he followed me down to the basement and made a pass. I told him to get lost.

"I suppose you think you're Queen Wanda?" he said grumpily when I made it clear I wanted nothing to do with him. He was referring to the legendary Queen Wanda of Polish history who drowned herself in the Vistula River rather than marry a German prince.

"No," I replied. "I'm only Wanda the potato scrubber. But I don't go with Germans either."

He left me alone after that. He could have sent me back to peeling potatoes, but I knew he wouldn't. Who would replace me? One of those women? Later on he also brought in the young girl. I didn't mind because she was nice. However, by now all the others were jealous, especially the two prostitutes. They were constantly making remarks about their "Jewish virgin." They didn't bother the other girl. She was just a kid, and her mother was still working with them. But they started on me and got nastier and coarser by the day. Real trouble was bound to start. I knew I had to get away from the whole pack of them . . . and soon!

On Monday I made my move. Nothing drastic—I simply stopped going to work. On Wednesday two SS soldiers with helmets and fixed bayonets came to my apartment and took me to the office of Scharfführer Meyers, the sergeant in charge of civilian workers. He was a serious man who was known for being strict but fair. He could have fired me right then, but because I had the reputation of being a good worker, he decided to give me the benefit of the doubt. He asked why I hadn't come to work, and when I failed to give him a good excuse, he punished me by demoting me to a lower job, one even lower than peeling potatoes. I was assigned to clean offices on the second and third floors.

This was a considerable step down. The pay was less, and I no longer received free meals. But at least I was away from those women. After a while I began liking the work. It was a much more interesting job. Before, I never got out of the kitchen. Now I went all over the building, seeing whatever was going on. When I first began, I was assigned to work with another girl. We started early in the morning before the soldiers ate breakfast. We had to work quickly because the floors had to be mopped before the men came to work. I hadn't been at it long when I made one of those unwitting slips. Each office had a sink. In one it was by the window instead of by the door. The other girl mopped that office the same way she mopped the others, from the window to the door. Then she carried the bucket back to the sink to empty it. I thought that was pretty stupid, lugging a dripping bucket of dirty water over a freshly mopped floor. When I began mopping that room I did it the other way around—from door to window. Then I emptied the bucket in the sink and tiptoed out. When the other girl saw me doing it that way she was amazed.

"Wanda, you work just like a Jew! Backwards!"

Oh, no, I thought. It's starting again. I knew that if I wanted to keep this job I would have to get away from her, too. After a while I saw my chance. She was a hard worker who always finished her half first, then nagged me to hurry up. One day I said, "I'm sorry, but this isn't working. You're always done before I am, and it's getting on my nerves. I don't want to slow you down or get in your way, so let's divide the rooms between us. You take half of them and I'll take the other half, and we'll each be responsible for doing our own."

That was fine with her and it was paradise for me. At last I could work by myself without worrying about someone watching my every move. I had music. Every office had a radio, and the first thing I did when I came in was turn it on. How the music lifted my day! I walked down the hallways with my bucket and mop, whistling and singing songs from operettas. I love to sing, though I can't carry a tune. For the first time in months I was actually enjoying myself. Sometimes I didn't finish on time, but it didn't matter. Nobody cared. The soldiers went on with their jobs while I worked around them. In time I got to know them, and one became my friend.

His name was Adrian. He was a sergeant like Meyers.

His job was making out the regimental payroll. I was cleaning his office with the radio on when he suddenly came in. He caught me completely by surprise. I was afraid he might punish me. Poles were forbidden to own or listen to a radio. But he didn't mind at all. He listened to the radio all the time while he worked, so what harm was there in my listening, too? We began talking, and he was quite surprised to find that I not only spoke German, but had attended a gymnasium. From then on I was no ordinary cleaning girl in his eyes. I was a person of culture and intelligence, someone worth talking to. We had long conversations about music, philosophy, and literature while he did the payroll and I mopped the floor. We often discussed Goethe because Adrian considered Goethe the greatest poet who ever lived. As a matter of fact, Adrian was a poet himself. He often worked on his poems when he should have been working on the payroll. He'd read me a few from time to time to see what I thought. They were quite good. Once he asked if I would like to make some money. He needed someone to do his washing. He offered to pay me in cigarettes, which were better than money because I could get a good price for them on the black market. I did such a good job that Adrian recommended me to his friends. Soon I was doing their washing, too.

Everything was working out beautifully. Instead of filthy talk and dirty looks, I had music, good conversation, and a nice little income on the side selling cigarettes to the neighbors.

All the cleaning women and kitchen workers wore big, robelike aprons over their clothes. Each worker had to supply her own. I didn't have an apron and couldn't afford to buy one, but I did have a lovely dressing gown with black and paisley stripes that was just the right length. Since its sleeves were too wide to work in comfortably, I pinned them up and it was perfect. Every evening before I went home I hung my gown in the women's dressing room in the basement. Then one morning I came to work and it was gone! What was I going to do? How could I replace it? Things like that were impossible to buy! I was determined not to make an issue of it no matter how upset I really was. I was certain one of the other girls had stolen it. I was even fairly sure which one: a dark, slender young woman named Kazia, very pretty and intelligent, who began working in the kitchen right after I left. Originally she came from a fine family and had even attended business college. She was the only one of the civilian workers other than myself who could speak fluent German. She was witty and vivacious. Everyone liked her. But she was a whore.

We were both the same size, so it would have fit her. And though now she owned nothing, she did have a taste for nice clothes. I was sure she took it, but what could I do? In my position I didn't dare make trouble. And, anyway, what proof did I have?

So I said nothing and went about my job in my street clothes. I was working in Adrian's office when he came in and noticed I wasn't wearing my robe. "Did something happen to it?" he asked.

"I guess somebody stole it over the weekend," I told him. "I hung it up in the dressing room when I went home, and this morning when I came to work it was gone."

I really wanted to forget about it, but Adrian was furious. "*Donnerwetter!*" he began to shout. "I'll find out who stole it! I'll teach them a lesson they won't forget!" I pleaded with him not to make a fuss, but he insisted. "We have all sorts of supplies lying around here. If they can get away with stealing your robe, soon they'll be stealing other things!"

He began an investigation immediately, storming downstairs to the kitchen shouting, "Who stole Wanda's robe? Just wait! I'll find out!" All the workers were questioned. Of course, nothing came of it. The robe was gone without a trace. But when Adrian was interrogating Kazia, she told him something—something I didn't find out about until much later.

There was a burglary at the battalion warehouse. Thieves broke in during the night and made off with a huge supply of bedsheets, pillowcases, and towels. Everybody was talking about it the next day. The investigators were certain it was an inside job. Nothing was forced or broken, so the culprits must have had access to a key and known when the guards went off duty. All civilian workers immediately came under suspicion. Adrian called everyone in for questioning, including myself. Only two people failed to provide good alibis. One was Stasiek the janitor. The other was Kazia. Both were locked up in basement cells while the officers decided what to do. Five days went by. No one knew if they would be shot or sent to a concentration camp. The other women begged me to plead with Adrian on Kazia's behalf. He would listen to me. I spoke German, and he was my friend. I promised to do what I could. I went down to the basement and spoke to Kazia through the bars. She gave me the details of her story, and I believed she was innocent. She might have taken my robe, but she wasn't a real criminal. I then went over to Adrian's office.

"Adrian, what do you want from Kazia?" I began to say. "She didn't steal anything. You know what a joker she is. She likes to kid around." I had a whole speech prepared, but he cut me off at once.

"I don't know why you're getting involved," he scoffed. "Why should you care if she rots in jail? She's no friend of yours. Do you know what she said to me when I was trying to find your robe? She said you were Jewish! That's right. She looked me right in the eye and said, 'You know, Wanda's a Jew!' And I told her if she ever opened her mouth about you again, she would get it from me!"

So that was it. Kazia figured out the truth and turned me in, but Adrian liked me too much to believe her. I took a deep breath to collect my thoughts. Then I said, "Well, you know what she's like. You know what she is." And it ended there.

But after that I always carried my papers and some money sewn in a belt which I wore under my clothes just in case I had to leave in a hurry.

A Summer
Interlude

It was a warm, beautiful Friday afternoon in mid-July 1943. I had just picked up my pay at the barracks and was walking home along the Vistula River. Kraków is an interesting city, one of the oldest in Poland, the first capital of the Polish kings. Although it is smaller that Warsaw and some of the other large cities in Poland, it is filled with churches and buildings, many dating back to the Middle Ages. The Wawel Palace overlooks the Vistula. The Jagielonski University is the oldest in Poland, while from the top of the Marjacka Spire of the cathedral the bugle call known as the Hejnał is sounded every day at noon. Walking was always my favorite recreation, and Kraków is a grand city to explore on foot. Now that the days were warm and sunny and the twilight did not come until late, I could indulge myself to the full.

On this particular day I was strolling past the Wawel Palace when just ahead I noticed a handsome young man walking arm-in-arm with a beautiful blonde woman. I looked again, this time more closely, and realized to my surprise that I knew him. No mistake about it—he was from Piotrków. He was fairly tall and had dark brown hair and pale blue eyes. He wore a mustache, which was un-usual among men his age, and dressed in riding boots and jodhpurs, which were considered very chic. And now here he was, just as I remembered him, strolling through the middle of Kraków with a Polish beauty on his arm. My instincts told me to pass him by, to take care of my business and let him take care of his. But, on the other hand, it had been so long since I had talked to anyone from home that I was curious. I simply had to find out what he was up to.

I followed him for a few blocks. He finally said good-bye to his girlfriend. I saw my moment and quickly ran up to him.

"Do you have a second? Can I talk to you?"

"Sure." He looked at me oddly. "Do I know you?"

"You may. Tell me, did you ever live in Piotrków?"

The sudden flash of fear in his eyes told me I had the right man. Now I had to give him a sign, some assurance he could trust me.

"You used to live on Szewska Street, didn't you?" I continued. "That's where I know you from. I had a girl-friend who lived on that street. Number Eight." Szewska Street was in the heart of the ghetto. Anyone with friends there had to be Jewish.

He caught on immediately. I could see his eyes brighten.

"Well, what do you know? There's someone else here from Piotrków. What a coincidence. We really ought to get together sometime and talk."

"I'd like that, too," I answered. "It's been so long since I've seen anyone from the old neighborhood."

We made a date to get together on Monday after I got off work. He was waiting for me on the corner, just as we arranged. We went walking down the boulevard together, no particular destination in mind, using the passing crowd as our cover as we spoke together in low voices. Here at last was a chance for me to take off the mask that by now seemed riveted to my face. Here was another human being to whom I could talk without hiding behind a façade, without worrying that the least slip of tone or inflection might give me away. He felt the same way. But even so, it took a while before he could bring himself to trust me. I asked how he was getting by. He told me he was involved in smuggling—exactly what, he didn't say. Then he asked me the same question.

"I'm working for the SS," I replied, and showed him my work card to prove it was true. He still found it hard to believe and pressed me to tell him more. But I had been around long enough to know better. The less people know about you, the better—even your friends. I thought he'd naturally understand that too, but he still persisted.

"Wouldn't it be easier for me to meet you at work?"

"Not on your life! Don't even think of doing it! It's nothing personal. I don't care one way or another. But I know the girls I work with better than you do. If they see you waiting for me, they're going to want to know who you are, where you live, how long we've been seeing each other, and why I don't introduce you to them. Don't you see? However innocently it starts, one thing leads to another and the whole business can easily get out of hand. It's trouble, and what do we need it for?"

He said he understood. But a few days later, when I came out the front gate, there he was in front of the barracks waiting for me. Not only that. He was flirting with the waitress from the officers' canteen! I was furious. What was he trying to do? Kill us both?

"Hi!" he said as I walked by. "I was waiting for you."

"Hi yourself," I said very angrily as I walked past. "What do you mean by coming here? You promised not to do it. How did you ever find the address?"

"Easy," he laughed. "I saw it when you showed me your work card."

"Very clever. Maybe you ought to work for the police because you're playing right into their hands. There's one rule I've always followed since I ran away from the ghetto, and you ought to follow it, too. Don't let the people at work know where you live, and don't let the people you live with know where you work. Understand? Mixing the two is just asking for trouble."

He apologized and promised not to show up at the barracks again. But I was beginning to have doubts about him. I already knew that he was apt to be reckless and that he wasn't very good at keeping promises. I considered ending the relationship right then, but in spite of my reservations I was so eager for a friend—a Jewish friend—that I was willing to give him another chance. I hoped he'd do better, because I needed someone desperately. The worst part of passing under false papers was that I was utterly alone. There was no one to turn to, no one to trust. I walked through a world of enemies with a deadly sword hanging over my head. For that reason, even a few moments of conversation with someone who shared my plight, who understood my hidden nightmares and sudden gut-wrenching chills, could make the terrors of my daily life that much easier to bear. For now, at least, I knew I was not the only Jew left alive. There was another with me, close by, a friend to whom I could turn. That simple knowledge meant a lot to me. I could not pass it by. But, I realized sadly, I might have to if he did something stupid again. I decided to wait and see.

We met on various street corners during the next few weeks. Our conversations seldom lasted more than an hour or two, but each time I learned a little more about him. Coincidences! He was living on Kurniki Street in the same building I lived in when I first came to Kraków. And guess who his landlady was? Mrs. Mokryjowa's sister, who lived with her mother in the apartment upstairs! As soon as I learned that, I knew we had to have a long talk.

"I know that building very well. I used to live there myself. Please—and I mean this very seriously—never ever tell anyone there that you know me. There is no reason why they have to know. To tell them is just asking for trouble."

He still couldn't understand why I was making a fuss, so I told him, "Some time ago a gentile gave me some excellent advice which I always follow. I'll share it with you. One Jew can blend in. Two are always suspect."

I wasn't sure whether the Mokryjowas suspected the truth about either of us. But the fact was that when my friend talked fast, he didn't pronounce the *cz* sound correctly. It came out slightly harder than a native speaking Polish would say it. Normally it wouldn't be noticed, but if people suspected he might be Jewish and decided to listen carefully, they couldn't help hearing it. One tiny slip like that was all it took to give a person away. That's why I didn't want anyone to know we were friends. If one of us went down, why drag the other down, too? He promised to do better in the future. I strongly hoped that he would.

How I looked forward to our walks together. From time to time we talked about ourselves, our families and friends, and how we came to be where we were now. We never discussed how we escaped from the ghetto or whom we left behind. Those memories were still too raw, too terrifying. Once upon a time we lived in Piotrków; now we were here. We ignored those blank spaces in our lives.

He came from a religious Hasidic family but shed his beard and earlocks when he grew older. Instead of studying to be a rabbi, he went to a trade school and learned to weave. Łódź, his hometown, was a large manufacturing city with the biggest textile industry in Poland, though most of the factories there were one-room workshops. He set up his loom in his parents' house and made a living weaving small items—socks and things like that—on consignment. Shortly before the war broke out he got married, and when the Germans expelled the Jews from Łódź, he came to Piotrków with his wife and parents.

Interestingly enough, as close as we were, I never knew his name. I have no idea what his Jewish name was because back home he was just a face I'd pass on the street. In Kraków we used our false passport names, and what his was I have long since forgotten. Let's call him Jasek because he looked very much like another boy I used to know by that name.

I looked forward to the times we spent together. There

were always small rowboats, canoes, and little kayaks tied up along the riverbank that people could rent for a small fee. That was what we often did. With our small boat far, far out in the middle of the river, we would sit for hours talking—really talking—pouring our souls out to each other without having to worry about being overheard. Jasek had a remarkable knowledge of Hebrew and Yiddish literature. He could go on for hours reciting Bialik and Peretz. It was extremely moving to listen to him. To this day I can hear his voice pouring out Bialik's "In the City of Slaughter," the famous poem written to commemorate the Kishenev pogroms of 1903.

> *Great is the sorrow and great is the shame*
> *And which of the two is greater?*
> *Answer thou, o son of Man . . .*

How those words struck like daggers into our hearts, for we were living not only in a city but in a world of slaughter.

Out on the river we would sit together through those warm summer afternoons, or else we picked our way along the bank, feeding the ducks, gathering wildflowers, looking for all the world like a pair of lovers. And any passerby who saw us must surely have thought that that was what we were—lovers. But we weren't. The words Jasek whispered in my ear weren't lovers' phrases. It was "In the City of Slaughter," or Peretz's stories, or the songs and legends of the Hasidic rabbis which he knew from his schooldays.

Don't misunderstand. Ours was a friendship—a Jewish friendship—and as such it was very important to each of us. But Jasek was not my boyfriend, and I was not his girl-friend. I drew that line at the beginning of our relationship, telling him all about Mayer and my feelings for him. I made it clear that I had no desire to get involved with anyone else. Besides, love affairs were a luxury I couldn't afford. Keeping alive from day to day was hard enough without romantic entanglements.

However, Jasek's views on that subject were completely different. He was an extremely handsome man, a ladykiller, and he took advantage of it. Polish women went crazy over him. The combination of dark hair and blue eyes was irresistible. Once he realized I was not going to be another conquest, he started telling me all about his different affairs. It was impossible to keep track of them all. He picked up one girl on the street, another in the park, another on the tramway—all in a single day. I wasn't impressed. After all, what was the point?

"I'm sorry, Jasek," I said after hearing the details of his latest liaison. "You may be older than me, but you don't understand anything about life at all. Can't you see that you're playing a dangerous game? You don't know these women like I do. I live and work with them. They talk. They talk about everything. How long will it take before one gets jealous? Don't you see? It's so easy for real trouble to start, and what do you need it for? Do you have to keep running around after women all the time? Don't you understand that we have only one duty to ourselves, one duty to the Jewish people, and that is to survive?"

He couldn't see it that way. He'd pick up a woman on the street or take up with some lonely spinster, moving from one to another like a monkey swinging from tree to tree. Many times I found his hedonism repulsive. "Hey!" I once blurted out, "what about your wife? Maybe she's dead, but you don't know for sure. Maybe she's not. Don't you ever think about her or wonder if you'll find her again?

What if you do? How will you face her after the way you've been living?"

He laughed in my face. "You don't have to worry about my wife. She'll take me back." I had nothing to say after that. It was a way of looking at life and treating people that was completely alien to anything I knew, and it made me uncomfortable. "Watch out, Jasek—you're playing with fire," was all I could say. But he wouldn't listen.

One special Sunday in August we went on a picnic. The women at work had told me about a certain park located just outside the city. It was beautiful, they said. I had never been there, and neither had Jasek, so we planned a special trip to see what it was like.

The park was huge. Little brooks and streams flowed through the forests and meadows. There were no benches or tables, but everyone brought picnic baskets and spread blankets on the grass. It seemed as if all Kraków were there. Groups of people were everywhere, singing, dancing, or just lying on the grass by the streams, enjoying the sound of flowing water and the brilliant sunshine.

We found a spot for ourselves away from the crowds. Lying back on our blanket, we could see the peaks of the Tatras, the highest mountains in Poland, forming a jagged edge along the horizon. The sight of those mountains brought back memories of when I was young, when I and all my friends spent a whole summer camping in the Tatras. I began telling Jasek about those times, about my experiences outdoors, how we had camped and hiked and slept out in the woods under the stars. He wanted to hear all about it because his childhood had been completely different.

Jasek had grown up indoors, in synagogues and yeshiva classrooms. My tales of life outdoors entranced him as much as his recitation of poems and stories moved me. So

A Summer Interlude

in a sense we each had something important to give to one another. That was what made our friendship so special. After the week-long strain of covering up my real identity, of putting up with constant vulgarity, I needed a time and a person with whom I could just be myself. My friendship with Jasek was the secret magic well from which I drew inner strength. Those who were in the concentration camps understand. If starving people think only of their hunger, they will go mad. They must try to remember the times when they weren't hungry. That was what our friendship meant to me: a reminder of who I really was. I am sure it meant the same to Jasek.

It was a good summer.

One day toward the end of summer Jasek came to me with some news.

"I moved," he said.

I asked where he was living now. I nearly gasped when he told me. I was appalled. But he thought it was a perfect setup.

He was renting a room in a three-room apartment. His landlady was a widow who lived there with her elderly mother. The widow was about thirty-five and gave the impression that her husband had died a few years before, though exactly what happened to him she never really said. A few weeks later there was a new development. "My landlady has a little store," Jasek told me. "She sells notions— you know, needles, spools of thread, stuff like that. Well, she's getting tired of running it by herself. She asked if I'd manage it for her. What do you think? Should I?"

"What do I think? Don't you know? Are you so blind you can't see where it's leading? You think she's just looking for a storekeeper? She's looking for a boyfriend, and that means trouble."

"Oh, no, no, no!" Jasek kept insisting. He didn't want to hear that. It was just a business arrangement—that was all. He started running the store, and it wasn't long before an affair started. Soon he was telling her about himself and about me, his good friend Wanda, whom he went to visit on Sundays. I was such a charming girl, he said. Since I was so charming, his landlady said she'd like to meet me, and soon Jasek was inviting me over to their house to get acquainted.

"What?" I exclaimed when I heard it. "Now I know you have lost your mind! You know I don't want to meet your girlfriends, and I certainly don't want to meet your landlady. I've told you a hundred times—one Jew is plenty, two is asking for trouble. You have your nerve even telling her about me. Stick your own neck in the noose if you want to, but leave mine out of it." I was furious, but that didn't seem to bother Jasek at all.

Needless to say, I never went over, but Jasek kept me informed. His landlady introduced him to one of her friends, a lovely woman who, with her little boy, came over one day for coffee. He described how they all sat together in the kitchen—the landlady, her friend, the little boy, and the landlady's old mother—and what a good time they had. I wasn't impressed.

Then one day Jasek announced that the landlady's birthday was coming up and they were all going to have a party. I was invited. I had to come. He had promised to bring me.

"You promised? Too bad. I'm not going. You know how I feel about that."

"Don't be so stubborn!" he pleaded with me. "There's nothing to be afraid of. If you don't come, everyone's going to be disappointed. They're all looking forward to finally meeting you."

"Nothing doing, Jasek! You know I want nothing to do with your lady friends. And if you're going to give me a hard time about it, then I'm not so sure I want to have anything to do with you. It's not that I'm stubborn. I'm trying to stay alive. I've been trying to show you how to stay alive, too, but you won't listen. You're looking for trouble, and sooner or later that's just what you'll get. Leave me out of it. I'm not going to your landlady's birthday party. And don't ever tell anyone else about me."

I didn't see him for two weeks after that. Then one day when I came home from work, my landlady met me at the door. "Miss Wanda," she said with a gleam in her eye. "We didn't know you had a boyfriend. We thought you were going with someone, but you never told us how handsome he is. He was just here looking for you."

"I don't know whom you're talking about."

"Sure you do. The guy with the mustache and the boots. Is he ever a killer!" He certainly was, in more ways than she suspected. I was furious. How did he find out where I lived? Probably the same way he found out where I worked—that one time I showed him my work card. I should have kept on walking that first time I saw him on the street and not said anything at all to him. By now it was clear he had no common sense, and his recklessness was putting me in danger.

"Did he leave a message?" I asked my landlady.

"Only that he'd meet you after work tomorrow."

Sure enough, the next day, when I came out the barracks gate, there he was. I walked straight toward him, determined to give him one final piece of my mind before breaking off our relationship right there. But as soon as I drew close enough to see his face, I realized something was wrong. Jasek was scared. Very scared.

"Something happened," I said. "Tell me."

"Let's walk." He took my arm, and as we went down the street, he told me the whole story. Three nights ago there was a knock on the apartment door. The landlady's mother opened it, and two men from the SD, the German security police, burst in. They knew exactly where to go. While one waited outside, the other came into his room without knocking.

"Get up and get dressed. You're under arrest. We've got you now, Jew, so just come along with us."

Jasek leaped out of bed. He got down on his knees before the policeman and begged for his life. "Have mercy. Please. I have money. Here is a whole roll of it. Marks, zlotys, American dollars. Take it all. It's yours. Just let me go. I'm only one poor Jew. You've killed thousands. What does one more or one less matter? Take my money. Take anything you want. No one will know. I won't tell. I promise. Just let me go. Please!"

The German smiled. He spoke softly with the soothing purr of a cat who has just come across a fledgling. "Hmmm. I like . . . the way you act. Perhaps . . . you might like . . . to work with us. Get off the floor. Here. Sit down. Now . . . let's talk this over . . ." Then he explained. Jasek's land-lady's husband had been a Jew. He was taken away when the Płaszów ghetto was formed and later shipped off to Auschwitz. Ever since then, the police kept the apartment under surveillance. After all, wouldn't a woman who was married to a Jew be likely to help other Jews? But how did they know he was Jewish? Jasek wanted to know. Can't anyone rent a room? The policeman laughed to himself. Remember the friend, the lovely lady who used to come by with her little boy? She was working for them. She was ferreting out Jews in hiding and turning them over to the secret police. The first time she saw Jasek—that day she came over for coffee—she put the finger on him. And the birthday party he wanted me to go to—she was there. Had I given into him and gone, I would have been lost.

"So you see," the policeman concluded. "She works with us . . . and so will you. That way . . . you will save your life." He told Jasek to come down to police headquarters in the morning so they could set him up to start working for them as a spy. Then the SD men left. Jasek didn't wait another minute. He moved out early that morning. He left his clothes, all his belongings, and ran.

"So where are you living now?" I asked.

"At my old place on Kurniki Street. Oh, I ran into your friend, Mrs. Mokryjowa. I said I knew you and that you told me you used to live there. She said you were very nice and to say hello."

I couldn't believe it! Even with the police on his trail, he still couldn't keep his mouth shut. By this time I was beyond giving lectures. Much more was at stake. What did I really know about Jasek? I asked myself. I knew that he was intelligent and daring, extremely charming when he wanted to be, and sensitive in many ways. But what did I really know about his character? Was he the type who could turn a friend over to the police to save his own skin? If so, I was in serious trouble. I had to find out where I stood, and I asked him directly, "Why did you go to Kurniki Street? Didn't you go to the police?"

He glared at me in shock and surprise. "Wanda, you are the last person I'd expect to ask me a question like that!

What do you think I am? Did you think I'd betray all the other Jews, and when there weren't any left, I'd turn you over, too? Do you really think I could be such a skunk?"

"No," I replied. "But I had to find out."

We walked on, trying to decide what to do. He already had a plan in mind. He was going to try to get to Lwów, then see about some way of slipping across the border into Hungary. It was a desperate gamble. Lwów was in the Ukraine. I knew a girl who had come from there. If survival was hard for a Jew in Kraków, in Lwów it was impossible. Jasek wanted me to come with him, but I refused.

"I have nothing to run away from. I'm not the one in trouble. Even if I were, I still wouldn't go with you. Not to Lwów. Not anywhere. Remember what I told you? Two Jews together just can't make it. Do what you have to do, but do it on your own."

I wished him luck, and that was the last I ever saw of him. He went to Lwów, and eventually I received a letter from him there. It was a beautiful love letter. I never believed he was capable of the emotions he expressed in it. He wrote that being away from me made him realize how much I meant to him. He told me how much he admired my sense of humor, my courage, my never-failing good sense. During the brief time we were together last summer, he didn't realize he was falling in love. He didn't think it could ever really happen to him, but it did. Now all his other girlfriends, all his other affairs meant nothing. He understood my feelings toward him and the fact that I already had a boyfriend. But even so, he had one wish. If he survived the war, he wanted to be able to meet Mayer some day and tell him how devoted and faithful I was. And, above all, he wanted to see me again.

A Summer Interlude

133

I received two more letters from Jasek after that. In the last one he wrote that he was about to carry out his original plan of slipping over the border into Hungary. He asked me to wish him luck and promised to write later if all went well. That was the last I ever heard from him.

I wish I could remember his real name.

The Kommandant

The officers' canteen was located on the first floor of battalion headquarters. It had its own staff consisting of a master chef, a waitress, and a janitress whose sole duty was keeping the room clean. No other civilian workers were allowed inside. One day Adrian called me from my regular duties and told me to report to the canteen at once. The janitress was out sick, and they needed someone immediately to get the room ready for lunch. As soon as I walked through the door, I realized why they didn't admit just anyone. What a contrast this was to the mess hall where the recruits ate! There were chandeliers on the ceiling, paintings on the walls, fine linen on the tables, gleaming silver and crystal everywhere. I set to work with my trusty mop and broom and apparently did an excellent job because from that time on, whenever an extra hand was needed in the canteen, I was the one they asked for. I felt like a recruit who was just selected to carry the banner in the big parade: no extra pay, but the prestige was enormous!

Soon afterward Sergeant Meyers summoned me to his office again. "Wanda," he said. "I have a special assignment for you." He issued me a new broom, a mop, a pail, an entire assortment of cleaning supplies, and took me outside to where a truck was waiting. After telling me to get inside, he nodded to the driver, who drove off at once. We finally stopped in front of an elegant apartment house in a very exclusive section of the city.

"Here we are!" the driver said. We got out, and I followed him into the building and upstairs to an empty apartment. "Clean it," he told me. "I'll come back for you at five."

I looked around. It was a big apartment. I couldn't possibly finish it in one day. "What if I'm not done?" I asked.

"We'll come back tomorrow or, if we have to, the next day. The important thing is to do a good job. A lot depends on it." Then he left.

It took a week before that apartment was thoroughly clean. I scrubbed it from floor to ceiling. Even the smallest corners were spotless. The driver picked me up at the barracks each morning and drove me back in the evening. We never spoke. Although I generally mind my own business, this time my curiosity got the better of me.

"What's going on? Who is this fancy apartment for?" I asked the driver one day as we were going back.

"Don't you know? This is going to be our Kommandant's apartment," he said with considerable pride. "He's bringing his wife from Germany, and this is where they're going to live."

That was interesting, but not really relevant to me. I went back to my regular job of cleaning offices, and everything went on as before. Then one day as I was wringing out my mop, a soldier in full battle dress came into the office where I was working.

"Are you Fräulein Wanda?" he asked gruffly.

"Yes," I said, wondering what he wanted. "I am Fräulein Wanda."

"Then come with me. You have been summoned to the adjutant's office."

The adjutant's office was on the next floor. The soldier escorted me upstairs. The adjutant was waiting for us at his desk. When I came in, he nodded and said something into the intercom. I heard someone reply. Then he said, "They are coming," and motioned to the soldier to take me in. Passing several empty conference rooms, we finally came to a tall, leather-upholstered door. The soldier stepped aside and showed me in.

I found myself in an immense, brilliantly lit office. One entire wall was made up of windows overlooking the Wawel Palace. Several long tables were covered with maps. Additional maps hung on the walls. The room was dominated by an enormous desk set right in the middle of the floor. Behind it, gazing out the window toward the Wawel, stood a tall officer with silver epaulets and jet black hair. He neither turned when I came in nor acknowledged my presence in any way, but continued staring out the window as if no one were there. As each minute passed, I grew more and more nervous, more and more frightened. Why was I summoned here? What did they want from me?

The Kommandant

137

"You can go," the officer finally said to the soldier, who clicked his heels, saluted, and left, shutting the door behind him. Then, still staring out the window, the officer began firing questions at me in rapid order like a drill sergeant shaking down a squad of recruits.

"How old are you? Do you have any relatives? Where do you live?"

I tried to collect my thoughts and answer each question, but all the while my knees were shaking. "It's all over," I thought. "He knows the truth. In another moment he will end this cat-and-mouse game and place me under arrest."

Then he asked, "Do you know anything about first aid, and if not, can you learn?"

"I don't have to learn, Sir," I replied, trying my best to sound calm. "I worked in a military hospital before coming here. I know all the different techniques for bandaging shoulders, elbows, knees, and heads."

"Interesting," he said. "Did they teach you that in the hospital?"

"No, Sir. I learned it in school. Everyone had to take a forty-eight-hour course in first aid."

"Very good," he nodded. "You can go."

He turned around to ring the bell on his desk, and for the first time since the beginning of the interview I saw his face. He was extremely handsome, but his eyes had a cold, ruthless glitter like those of a bird of prey. His head seemed strangely small in contrast to his height and immense shoulders. In a way it reminded me of something I once saw in a museum—a Roman bust of a little boy's head that by some accident had been attached to the torso of a full-grown man. Then the soldier came and escorted me back downstairs, and without requesting or receiving any explanation, I picked up my mop and went back to work.

Normally I would have forgotten the whole episode. As in the case of the apartment, I was often sent here or there or assigned various tasks without being told why. But something about this incident was different and especially puzzling. I knew one thing: my secret was still safe. Then what was this all about? High-ranking officers have better things to do with their time than bother cleaning women. I pondered the matter for a few days and decided I simply had to know. So I went to Sergeant Meyers, who was always friendly to me, and asked what was going on.

He laughed. "Remember that apartment I sent you to clean? That was for Colonel Roemer, our Kommandant. He was the one who called you upstairs. He's bringing his wife here from Germany and wanted to know if we had any Polish girl on the staff suitable to be taken into a German home as a maid. He was very explicit. He didn't want any drinkers, smokers, or flirts. Well, Adrian and I put our heads together and immediately came up with you. 'It has to be Wanda!' we both said. 'There's nobody else around here like that!' When we gave him your name, he asked who you were. 'The one who goes around murdering the operettas!' we told him."

So! The Kommandant knew all about me from the first.

A few days later Sergeant Meyers summoned me to his office again. "Wanda, I have another special assignment for you. Tomorrow morning when you come to work, wait outside by the gate. A chauffeur will pick you up and drive you to the Kommandant's apartment. Mrs. Roemer will be there. Stay as long as she needs you, and when you're done, the chauffeur will bring you back."

The Kommandant

Sure enough, at seven o'clock the next morning a staff car came by and picked me up. On the way over we stopped at the flower market, where the chauffeur told me to buy as many flowers as I needed to decorate the apartment properly. I was in heaven. I love flowers, and here I had carte blanche to buy as many as I liked.

I arrived at the apartment in a chauffeur-driven Mercedes piled high with flowers. The chauffeur helped me carry the flowers upstairs. Then he left to fetch Mrs. Roemer from her hotel. In the meantime I was to arrange the flowers and have everything ready when she arrived.

The apartment was bare when I last saw it. Now it was elegantly furnished with elaborately carved antique furniture. I walked through the rooms arranging flowers in every vase. I pretended that this was my own apartment, my own beautiful furniture, my own beautiful flowers.

In the midst of my daydream the doorbell rang. I ran to get it and found myself greeting a young woman slightly older than myself, not especially pretty, and rather plainly dressed with her hair cut in a sporty, rather severe fashion. She wore no makeup, not even lipstick. As for her bearing, it was definitely self-assured, but quite pleasant and not at all haughty.

"Oh, you must be the girl from the barracks," she said as she entered, glancing quickly about the apartment. "I like the way you arranged the flowers. I am Thea Roemer."

I took her coat, and together we set to work. After rearranging some of the furniture, Mrs. Roemer decided to bake some cookies. While she mixed the batter, I prepared the oven. When it was ready, I took out the cookie sheet and greased it. Mrs. Roemer dipped out the batter, but when she tried to put the sheet back into the oven, it wouldn't fit.

"What are we going to do?" she asked, very perplexed. "This cookie sheet doesn't fit in the oven. I can't understand it. It fit before."

"Maybe it has something to do with that law of physics," I suggested, "remember, the one that says heated objects expand? When the oven was cold, the cookie sheet fit without any trouble, so perhaps we should wait for it to cool again before putting it in."

She stared at me. "Where did you learn that?"

A slip! Since when do cleaning women start spouting the laws of physics? The truth was out, so there was no point in trying to cover it up again.

"In the gymnasium," I said.

"Oh? So you went to a gymnasium?" And that was the beginning of our friendship.

Over the next few weeks a definite routine began to develop. I reported to the barracks in the morning, signed in, and waited for the chauffeur to take me to the apartment. There I helped Mrs. Roemer with various chores until late afternoon. Then the chauffeur picked me up and brought me back to the barracks, where I finished the day cleaning offices or seeing to other tasks. However, as the weeks rolled by, I found myself spending more and more time with Mrs. Roemer and less and less time at headquarters.

One morning Mrs. Roemer took me aside and explained that from now on I would be spending the entire day with her. Then she let me in on a secret. She was pregnant. Since she had a history of miscarriages, her husband was taking no chances. He brought her to Kraków to keep an eye on her and make sure she received the finest medical care. The doctor ordered her to stay in bed for the entire first month. Since Colonel Roemer was always at work, someone was obviously needed to look after Mrs. Roemer and run the household. That someone was going to be me.

I was delighted with my good fortune and thrilled for her, for by now Mrs. Roemer and I were very close friends. She was a lovely person: intelligent, kind, attractive in her own way, and extremely gentle. In many ways she was the older sister I never had. I often felt sad for her because she was so very lonely. At home in Magdeburg she had her family and friends for company, but here in Kraków her only companion was her maid. And she had Colonel Roemer for a husband!

Except for the fact that he was extremely handsome and looked like a god in uniform, I could never understand how such a sweet, lovely person as Mrs. Roemer could marry a monster like that. He was a horror as a human being. Everyone at headquarters was terrified of him. He had a vicious temper, and heaven help the unlucky soldier whose uniform was wrinkled or who failed to carry out an order to the letter! But he was a courageous officer. Once on the Russian front he held an entire section of the line against a massive Soviet attack. He refused to retreat, even when directly ordered to do so. The line held, but only four men survived out of the whole battalion. Roemer was nominated for the Ritter Cross, the highest German decoration.

But whatever Colonel Roemer's merits as an officer, his credentials as a husband left much to be desired. He was an alcoholic. He maintained a huge personal stock of the finest brandies and liqueurs and could sail through half a dozen bottles in an evening. But I never saw him drunk or even slightly tipsy. As for tenderness and concern, such emotions were beneath him. Colonel Roemer was the perfect SS man even in his domestic life. I frequently had the feeling that Mrs. Roemer was not so much a companion as a status symbol—a young, cultured wife from a socially prominent family fit in nicely with the big automobile, the fancy apartment, the beautiful furniture. Her job was to supervise an elegant home and provide children to further her husband's career. She was also expected to know her place. Mrs. Roemer would often go through the trouble of preparing a lovely dinner only to have her husband not show up. His excuse? He was busy at the office. He never thought to call. However, when she once removed a serving dish from the wrong side, he refused to speak to her for four weeks. He was a horrible man. I couldn't stand him.

Several months passed, and Mrs. Roemer's pregnancy was beginning to show. Although she was now allowed out of bed, she felt very unattractive and abandoned. Except for me she was alone, and so we talked together for hours, discussing everything from Schiller to Nietzsche. It was heavenly for me because I was starved for intelligent conversation. I made the beds to classical music and washed the dishes to philosophical discussions as the days flew by. But because he knew nothing about those topics, it annoyed Colonel Roemer no end to hear our discussions. He was left out, and that made him angry. Once he exploded at the dinner table while Mrs. Roemer and I were preparing the meal.

"*Donnerwetter!* Must I eat burnt food because you and Wanda have those damned philosophical discussions in the kitchen?"

On other occasions he would say, "You and Wanda lie under one featherbed," implying that we were conspiring against him in some way. But most often, if we were talking about a concert or a play, we would turn around and find him standing silently in the doorway, scowling.

When Mrs. Roemer was in her eighth month, an old friend of the colonel's came from Prague for a visit. Mrs. Roemer cooked an exquisite dinner although it was foolish, not to say dangerous, for her to be out of bed in her condition. I stayed long past quitting time to help her serve and clean up afterward. By then it was very late. Since Mrs. Roemer was exhausted, Colonel Roemer and his friend decided to continue the party at the officers' canteen back at headquarters. I only lived a few blocks from the barracks, and the two men volunteered to drop me off on the way. As we were driving back, I overheard Colonel Roemer tell his friend about a young mistress he had in town. They were going there for another party after they dropped me off. I was shocked. How could he go to another woman after his poor wife worked so hard to entertain *his* friend? Such vile, selfish behavior was beyond me. But I was only the maid. I kept my mouth shut.

The next day when I came to work, I found Mrs. Roemer frantic. Where was Kurt? He hadn't come home. She was so upset I was afraid she might have a miscarriage. I hurriedly calmed her down. "It's nothing," I said. "Don't worry. I used to clean up those staff offices. Believe me, once a party gets going, it can go on all night." I told a little white lie—but for her sake, not his.

The Nazis always stressed the need to produce strong healthy children. For that reason a special course in infant and child care was offered to all German expectant mothers. Since I was going to be responsible for the baby's care, special arrangements were made for me to attend in Mrs. Roemer's place.

Sitting in a classroom with the pampered wives of high

German officers and officials was an interesting experience. It was an excellent course. We learned all about babies: how to diaper them; how to hold them; how to feed and burp them. We also learned how to prepare formula. This was especially important for me, for while most women were encouraged to breast-feed, Mrs. Roemer was simply not up to it.

It was easy to see what was happening. Upper-class women did not raise their children themselves. I was going to be the nanny, not just for this baby but for all the other little Roemers I was sure the colonel had planned. By enrolling me in the course he was making certain I knew what to do. Slowly but surely I was becoming a very important member of that household, which was fine with me. I had the perfect job and, in Mrs. Roemer, the perfect employer. I only hoped it would last.

Gestapo on My Trail

The summer of 1943 passed, and that beautiful season the Poles call *babie lato* came. It was the last breath of summer, the brief final outpouring of warmth and light before the coming of fall. It is a time of year whose moments stand out clearer than any other, perhaps because they are inevitably tinged with sadness. The gardens and meadows, so fragrant and richly hued, will soon be barren, chilled by the icy pallor of the winter sun. During this season I find my moods constantly changing. One day I am exhilarated and alive, bursting with hope and laughter. The next finds me very blue.

I was still living on Ditla Street, sharing an apartment with three other tenants: the old landlady, her young grandson, and another old woman who worked as a laundress in a hotel. During this time I received letters from Piotrków regularly—from my father, from Mayer, from Renia. They came by way of a sympathetic Polish girl who picked them up in the ghetto and mailed them outside. Since the laundress and the landlady were both illiterate, I felt no need to hide my mail. I kept my letters in my nightstand drawer, and every night, whenever I felt that aching loneliness, I took them out and read them over and over again, line by precious line. I really didn't have to read them. I knew each one by heart. Still, the simple act of reading just a few words or even holding the paper in my hand was enough to make me feel better. Not happy. Those letters were far from happy. But even so, they were a connection, however frail and thin, with my other life, my other self that still existed.

I had other papers in my drawer as well: my medical insurance book, a few photos of myself for official documents, and a picture of Mr. and Mrs. Banasz and their dog. Not that I felt especially sentimental about them, but in that picture they both looked extremely Polish and I used it as part of my cover. I told people they were my aunt and uncle.

I am a very fastidious person by nature, and it bothers me when things are not where they belong. That drawer was a mess. Letters, photographs, documents were all strewn about. I knew I ought to straighten it up, but somehow I never got around to doing it. Still, it bothered me. If nothing else, I knew I should at least do something about those letters. It was foolish to leave them lying around. I should either destroy them or hide them somewhere where they would be safe. One Thursday night I decided not to put it off any longer. I sorted out the letters and photographs, locked them up in my suitcase, and put the suitcase in the closet. All that was left in the drawer was my medical insurance book.

The next day—Friday—was payday. Mrs. Roemer always let me off early on Friday so I could get back to the barracks in time to pick up my pay. I am a person of regular habits. I am that way now, and I was that way then. A person could set his watch by me. At 6:00 A.M. I went to work. At 5:00 P.M. I came home. At 6:30 I visited with the neighbors. And at 9:00 I went to bed. Spring, summer, fall, winter—it never varied. But after collecting my pay on this particular Friday, I had a vague sensation of uneasiness, a sensation hard to describe except as a sharpened awareness of myself and my surroundings. I couldn't imagine why that should be.

It was a day like any other. I was walking my regular route along the Vistula and about to turn down Ditla Street to go home when suddenly I had a strong premonition— almost a warning—that it wasn't time to go home. Not yet. I continued along the river thinking to myself, "Today I think I'll walk all the way to the bridge just to see how long it takes to get there." I got to the bridge and walked across to the far side. By then my feet were tired, so I sat down by the riverbank to rest. As I sat there, catching my breath, I saw the spiders spinning their webs among the wild roses. In my mind, too, I spun a web, one of glistening sunlight, to catch these last precious moments of summer. For a while I watched the insects at work. Then I got up and continued walking.

I remembered my family and friends, the love and happiness we shared, turning those golden memories over and over again like the pages of a well-loved book. "Where are they all now?" I wondered. "Are they even alive? What has happened to them? What will happen to me?"

When I finally stopped and looked around to see where I was, I found that I had walked all the way out to Płaszów, one of the city's suburbs. It was still light out, but I had lost all track of time. I glanced at my watch. Was it seven o'clock already? I had no idea it was that late. I turned around and hurried home.

As I came down Ditla Street, I saw the landlady's grandson standing on the balcony waving to me. "Miss Wanda! Miss Wanda!" he called out. "A soldier was just here! He was looking for you!"

"Really?" I wasn't too concerned. It was probably someone from the barracks. I shrugged and went inside. The landlady was waiting for me. I could see she was very upset.

"Miss Wanda, where have you been all this time? A soldier was here waiting for you. He was here from two o'clock until six. He kept asking me when you were coming home. I told him you always come at five, but you didn't come. Where were you?"

That was none of her business. "What did he look like?" I asked.

"He had a steel helmet, and he wore a black uniform. Oh, he also left this note for you." She gave me the note. I opened it. It read: "Will Fräulein Wanda Gajda please come at eight o'clock tomorrow morning to Room 107 at the Geheimespolizei-SD office on Montelupich Square?"

Geheimespolizei-SD! A chill ran up my spine. This was no routine assignment from the barracks. It was the Gestapo, the dreaded secret police. I could imagine why they might want to speak with me. However, I decided not to make a move until I had a better picture of the situation. I took the note to my friends on the second floor. I explained that a soldier had come to my apartment while I was away and asked my landlady all sorts of questions about me. Before leaving, he gave her this note.

"Wait a minute," my neighbor said. "I know a policeman who lives in this building. Let's show the note to him. He'll know what it's all about." So together we went to the policeman's apartment and showed him the note. He looked at it briefly and scratched his head.

"One-oh-seven? That's the Political Department. What do they want with you?"

What he didn't realize, but what I knew perfectly well, was that Jews came under the Political Section. I needed all my self-control to keep from panicking. How the secret police learned about me I didn't know. Perhaps they cracked an underground cell, or maybe someone at work turned me in. There were a hundred possibilities, but all that mattered now was that I vanish as soon as possible. I ran upstairs and grabbed one of my two suitcases from the closet. Fortunately they were both packed for just such an emergency. My neighbor promised to watch it while I went back for the other one, but my landlady wouldn't give it to me.

"Nothing doing!" she shouted. "What if the police come back and say I let you get away with everything? I'm not going to jail for you!" She wouldn't let me take my featherbed or pillow either. What could I do? There wasn't time to argue. I left everything and ran.

What now? Terror twisted my insides into knots, making it hard to breathe. My palms were wet, and my heart was as heavy as my suitcase. "Don't lose your head. Keep a grip on yourself," I kept thinking over and over again. I did, but it wasn't easy. I thought I had finally reached a haven with a good apartment and a perfect job. Now the running and hiding were about to start all over again.

In the Mouth of the Wolf

Even though I was in grave danger, I knew that if I could keep my wits I had a chance. The secret police hadn't caught me yet. If I could get through the next three days—if I could collect my thoughts, assess the situation, and make some alternate plans—I knew I would be all right. But I had to have those three days. The working hours were no problem. I doubted the police would find me at Mrs. Roemer's because the neighbors only knew that I worked "somewhere in the military." But where would I sleep now that I could no longer go back to my apartment? I had one idea, at least for that night. While I was working in the kitchen, I made friends with another civilian worker—Mr. Kowalski. He and his wife invited me over to their apartment several times, and I often slipped them vegetables and other foodstuffs from the kitchen. Now that I was working for Mrs. Roemer I didn't see them as much, but we were still friends. I decided to pay the Kowalskis a visit.

They were delighted to see me. We sat down and began talking, and soon it was eight o'clock. I knew perfectly well that curfew was at eight, but I let the conversation continue until a quarter to nine. Then I suddenly looked at my watch and cried, "Jesus Maria! I was having such fun I forgot all about the time. It's way after curfew! How am I going to get home?"

"Wanda, don't worry!" they laughed. "You'll spend the night here." Which is just what I intended to do.

By next morning my plans were set. I had to get out of Kraków—preferably out of Poland. I could have simply disappeared, but I didn't want to do that. I wanted the break to be clean, without any loose ends to possibly trip me up in the future. The easiest way to do that was to volunteer for labor service in Germany.

Mrs. Roemer once asked me about my family. I told

her I was an orphan, that my mother died when I was small, and that my father subsequently drank himself to death. That was the reason I never wanted anything to do with liquor, having personally experienced the damage it could do. As for the rest of my family, my only relatives were a younger brother and sister still living in Piotrków. My sister was married to a policeman.

When I came to work in the morning, I asked Mrs. Roemer if I could have the next three days off. I explained that I had just received a letter from my sister. My brother was in trouble, and I had to go home immediately. Mrs. Roemer raised no objection. In fact she told me to take more time if I thought I needed it, especially since I hadn't used any of the vacation time due me. I thanked her and said good-bye, promising to return in three days. It was all I could do to keep from crying. I loved this job, and I adored Mrs. Roemer. Yet in my heart I knew I was saying good-bye for the last time. I was never coming back.

I took the next train to Częstochowa and went directly to the Central Labor Office. There was a special section for Poles applying for labor service. I had all my documents ready. There was a long line, so I had to wait. My turn came shortly before noon. Stepping up to the desk, I said to the clerk, "I'd like to go to Germany. Do you have any good contracts available?"

"As a matter of fact we do," he said. "A whole batch of new ones just came in this morning. The only problem is the boss went out to lunch a minute ago, and we can't process you until he returns. Can you come by at one?" I was about to leave when he called me back. "Tell you what. As long as you're here, let me look over your papers."

I handed over my documents for him to examine. He was leafing through them when all of sudden he exclaimed.

"You came here from Kraków? What in the world for? The main Central Labor Office is *in* Kraków. They have all the best jobs there. What are you doing here?"

It was a slip, and I had to cover it quickly before he figured out that I might be on the run. "Oh, it's a long story," I said, snatching back my papers. "I'll come back after lunch and tell you all about it." But I never went back. Instead I got on the next train and continued on to Piotrków, where I spent the next two nights with Mrs. Banasz. When I felt sure of myself, I went back to Kraków, applied for a contract at the Central Labor Office there, and got a job in a factory in Leipzig.

As I was going through the process of filling out different forms and undergoing various physical examinations, I struck up a conversation with one of the young women waiting in line with me. Everyone is naturally a little nervous in such situations, so it's fairly easy to become friends with a stranger in a very short period of time. We went through all the procedures together, and by the time they were over, anyone who saw us would have thought we were lifelong companions. As we were sitting in the waiting room waiting for the final word on when our tickets would arrive, the supervisor of the women's section of the Central Labor Office came over and sat down next to us. He was a Pole, not a German, and he seemed friendly enough. He asked if we were excited about going to Germany together.

"We're not really going together," we told him. The other woman was going to work on a farm with her sister, and I was going to that factory in Leipzig.

"You mean you just met? You didn't know each other before?"

We told him we just met today for the first time. He thought that was interesting. Then he turned to me. "I hate to tell you this, but Leipzig is a very bad place. You'll probably end up working in a munitions factory, and those installations are being bombed all the time. You're not really going to Leipzig, are you?"

"Yes," I insisted. "That's what they told me."

"Tell you what. When you finish up here, come over to the main office and see me."

"What for? I thought I was all done?"

"That's true," he agreed. "But it's just that you seem like a nice person, and I'd like to do you a favor. Take it from me. You don't want to go to Leipzig. Let me see if I can't get you a better job."

How could I argue? For all I knew, perhaps he was right about Leipzig. In any case the secret police were combing the city for me right now. My only chance was to get to Germany . . . and soon! After the Labor Service officials finished our processing, I went around to the main office. Sure enough, the supervisor was expecting me. He showed me into his office, asked me to sit down, and began going through my papers.

"Hmmm. It says here you have a job in Kraków working for the SS. Then why do you want to go to Germany?"

I had a story all prepared. "It's because of a broken heart. My fiancé and I were supposed to be married in August, but just at the last minute he ran off and left me. I've been humiliated. I simply can't take living in this town anymore. I want to get as far away as I can." I took out my handkerchief to wipe my eyes, but I was watching his reactions the whole time. He nodded sympathetically, but I could tell from his look that it wasn't working. He was on to me. He hadn't called me here just be get me another job—he suspected that I was Jewish. Very well, then. Let's see who would outwit whom. To my surprise I wasn't frightened at all. No. I was angry. How dare he suspect me! I hadn't come this far to be caught now. The next move was his. I waited to see what he'd do.

For a while he didn't say anything. Then he leaned back in his chair and absentmindedly began whistling "Ave Maria." As if only Catholics knew "Ave Maria"! It was a well-known melody—Mayer used to play it on his violin. This fellow would have to do a lot better than that to catch me. Suddenly he stopped whistling and leaned forward.

"Strange. I forgot what I was whistling."

"You mean 'Ave Maria'?" And I began singing it for him.

"Ah, yes. That's right. 'Ave Maria.' How could I forget?" We talked about that and other things for a while. He told me he could understand why I felt I had to get away from Kraków. He, too, had left his hometown for a similar reason. "You know, you're like a Jewish girl," he suddenly said right in the middle of the conversation. "You're quick. You think fast."

My life depended on my reply, but I was ready. Here was where all the dirty, vulgar talk I heard in the kitchen finally stood me in good stead. I used it now, and I used it well.

"Well, to tell you the truth," I laughed. "The kids in school used to tease me about that all the time. You see, my mother once worked as a maid in a Jewish house. How do I know who 'made' me? My baptismal certificate says that "Gajda" is my father's name, but who knows?"

He laughed, too. Then the door behind us opened and another man came in. The supervisor introduced us. "Meet Miss Gajda. She has applied to go to Germany. She'll probably be leaving in a few days." The other man muttered a few polite words, then turned to the supervisor, shook his head, and left as quietly as he entered.

The supervisor turned back to me and said: "Ever since I started working here, I've seen so many Jews come through this office that I wouldn't be surprised if there were more Jews in Germany now than there are in Kraków. That fellow I just introduced you to is a Ukrainian. He and I work together, and believe me, there isn't a Jew in the world he can't sniff out! Just to give you an idea, a few weeks ago a fellow came in—tall, blond, blue eyes—a sailor in the Merchant Marine. He said he wanted to go to Germany to work, but we smelled him out right away. I knew he was a Jew, but I didn't let on. The night before they leave, the workers sleep here in a guarded barracks. I made sure this sailor was assigned to a bunk on the third floor. I went to him that night and told him I knew what was up. Did he plead! He got down on his knees and begged me not to give him away. He gave me every zloty he had, his watch, even his rings. I told him not to worry. I promised to take care of his papers and send them on through. But that dirty Jew didn't trust me. When I went up the next morning, the window was open and he was gone. Imagine! From three stories up—gone! How do you like that?" Not one wisp of emotion crossed my face.

"I don't know how he does it, but that Ukrainian never makes a mistake. We've been working together for over a year now, and believe me, none of them gets by. He spots 'em just like that! They can't fool him!"

I shrugged. "Is that all? You brought me here just to tell me stories? I thought you were going to get me another job."

"Unfortunately no," he apologized. "I may as well tell

you the truth. I had my suspicions about you. It started when you told me that you just met that other girl today. That's how those Jews operate. Whenever they're in a crowd, they always try to latch onto someone so they won't be noticed. I invited you over here so my partner could have a look at you. But he tells me you're clean."

"You bet," I said as I got up to leave. "I'm no Jew."

A close call, but I didn't dare rest. Now my immediate challenge was to get through the next three days. By then my tickets would arrive, and I would be off to Germany. I worked at Mrs. Roemer's during the day and spent the first night with a girl I knew. I spent the second with the illiterate Ukrainian from the kitchen, the one with the baby. She tried to talk me into moving in with her permanently, but I wanted no part of that. Besides, in another day I would be gone.

On the morning of the third day I checked in at the Central Labor Office. Sure enough, the final papers and tickets had arrived. One by one the clerk called out the names of the volunteers in alphabetical order, and each one stepped forward to receive his or her contract. I waited for my name, but the clerk skipped right over it. What happened? There must be some mistake.

"No mistake," the officials told me. My contract had simply not been approved.

"But why?" I asked.

They explained. On my application I listed the SS as my present employer. The needs of the SS took precedence over every other department, so before I could be cleared to go to Germany, Colonel Roemer, my present employer, had to release me. He refused. What was I to do now? I felt utterly lost and helpless. Pulling myself together, I decided the best thing to do was go back and have a talk with him. Perhaps I could persuade him to let me go.

"Colonel Roemer, why are you doing this to me?" I pleaded. "I was all set to go to Germany. I filled out all the forms and passed the physical. All I needed was my contract. But you won't let me go. Now what am I going to do? My landlady already rented out my bed to someone else. I have no place to live, no place to sleep. Where am I going to stay?"

"I don't understand you at all," he replied, quite flustered. "Anyone would think I was doing you a favor. Why on earth do you want to go to Germany? Don't you know what those factories are like? Aren't you happy here?"

"I'm very happy here," I answered. "But that's not the point. It has nothing to do with you or Mrs. Roemer. I have to leave for personal reasons." I explained that I had had a big quarrel with my sister while I was in Piotrków and simply wanted to get as far away as possible. I declined to discuss it further.

Colonel Roemer threw up his hands. "Maybe my wife can talk some sense into you. I certainly cannot!"

Shortly afterward Mrs. Roemer approached me and asked what was wrong. I told her my sister's husband, the policeman, made advances to me while I was staying in their house. My sister became very jealous and accused me of trying to steal him from her. I was so shocked and hurt that now I wanted to run away from it all and disappear. The best way to do that was to go to Germany.

"I understand," said Mrs. Roemer, "but I doubt that running away is the answer. Besides, I need you here. What would I do without you, now with the baby coming? As for finding a place to live, you won't have to. Kurt and I will be moving to another apartment soon. This one is too far from the center of town. The new apartment has a maid's room just behind the kitchen. You can have that room if you like and live with us."

I agreed reluctantly—at least on the surface. Inside I was overjoyed. Mrs. Roemer didn't realize it, but she just handed me my life. Especially since I knew a few facts about bureaucratic procedure. All Poles were required to register in the official ledger of the apartment building where they lived. Germans, on the other hand, had only to register with the Civil Administration downtown. I stayed with the Roemers until they moved, and then I didn't register at all. No one asked me to! In fact Mrs. Roemer didn't know that the requirement for Poles existed.

Thus, as far as official records were concerned, my last known address was on Ditla Street. Then I disappeared. The police were looking for me high and low, and there I was, four blocks away from my last address, sharing an apartment with the SS Kommandant of Kraków! I was living in the wolf's mouth now, and, believe me, there is no better refuge in the world.

Scenes
from the
Hurricane's
Eye

Within the most ferocious storm lies a center of eerie calm known as the eye of the hurricane. Raging winds swirl about, uprooting trees, obliterating everything in their path. Yet within the eye of the storm there is not a single breeze. The sky is clear. The sun shines. Thus it was with my life with the Roemers. While armies collided in earth-shaking combat, bombs blasted cities to bits, and trains rolled on schedule to guarded camps where blackened chimneys belched greasy smoke day and night, I dusted, went shopping, served dinner. It was a normal life. Abnormally so.

The baby was due any time. Over these last difficult months Mrs. Roemer and I had become very close. By now

I was more than a maid; I was a helper, a confidante, a friend. From time to time she would say to me, "Wanda, it's very strange. You're not like other Polish girls at all. You're much more like a German." That was a great compliment. In effect Mrs. Roemer was telling me that I was an intellectual equal, a quality she never expected to encounter in someone who was only a servant. I often wondered if it were wise to stand out like that, but I really had no choice. I never could play the role of a dunce. It was simply not in me. And while I was always respectful and conscientious about my work, I refused to be a flunky. I let no one intimidate me—not even Colonel Roemer.

One morning while I was serving breakfast, a sudden breeze blew the balcony door shut. The bang startled everyone. The colonel was furious. *"Donnerwetter!"* he roared. "Can't you take care of that?" I set down the serving dish, shut the door, and left the dining room. "Well? Can't you at least say '*Jawohl*'?" he shouted after me. I went straight to my room without replying or turning around. Later, when Mrs. Roemer came to smooth things over, as she always did, I explained my feelings to her.

"Mrs. Roemer, please tell your husband that I am not one of his dumb recruits. I do not say '*Jawohl*'!"

My pride intrigued Colonel Roemer, especially when he realized I was not afraid to stand up to him. He constantly tried to bait me to see if I would back down. He used to start in at the dinner table or late in the afternoon when I served tea.

"Ah, look at this! That's the Polish way of doing things!" he'd comment with scorn. "Slovenly! Inefficient! Disorganized! Such a stupid, insignificant country has no right to exist. After Germany wins this war, we'll swallow

Scenes from the Hurricane's Eye

161

Poland up, just as she deserves. Poles! What a gang of idiots! So incompetent, so stupid!"

While I personally had little love for Poland myself, my outward posture was always that of a patriot. I refused to let Colonel Roemer browbeat me. Very patiently I answered, "Colonel Roemer, what do you expect me to say? Poland may not be as big or as important as Germany, but it is my motherland and I love it."

There was no point in the argument, but since I always answered back, Colonel Roemer took a liking to me. He might try to bait me, but he treated me with respect all the same. As he frequently said to his wife, "Wanda has pride." And pride was a quality he admired, even in a servant.

My false papers gave my birthday as December 12. I never thought anything of it, first of all because it wasn't really my birthday and second because it is the custom in Catholic countries to celebrate a person's saint's day, the day sacred to the saint after whom one is named, rather than the birthday. Nevertheless, the Roemers made note of the date and planned a surprise party. Mrs. Roemer baked a special cake with brandy just for the occasion. I was in my room reading, not expecting a thing, when they asked me to come to the living room.

"Well, Wanda," Colonel Roemer said after inviting me to sit down, "today is your birthday, and we want you to celebrate." I opened my present. It was a small bottle of 4711, a nice German cologne. Mrs. Roemer used it herself, and I liked it very much. Then we cut the cake, which was delicious. We laughed and talked for a while. To crown the occasion, Colonel Roemer insisted I have a glass of brandy. He took one of his shot glasses, filled it nearly to the brim, and made me drink it down in one swallow. I never drank hard liquor, so finishing that one glass was not easy. The colonel noticed my discomfort and decided to have some fun.

"Since this is such a special occasion, Wanda, you must have another drink." He poured out a second glass. I hardly finished that when he poured me a third. By now Mrs. Roemer could see that the joke had gone too far and that I was in considerable distress.

"Let her go, Kurt. She's had enough."

But Colonel Roemer was enjoying himself too much to let me go just yet. I had to finish the third drink. Then he poured a fourth. I clutched the edge of the table to keep from falling. My head was reeling and my knees felt weak. Nevertheless my mind was clear. "You must be extremely careful now. Your life is on the line. Watch what you say. Every single word," I thought to myself. One Yiddish word substituted for a German one or the slightest hint of a Jewish accent and I was lost. My mind remained alert that whole time. But after the seventh drink, when Colonel Roemer finally gave me permission to leave, I found I couldn't move. My body was totally disconnected from my brain. My arms and legs refused to budge. Mrs. Roemer had to help me to my room, undress me, and put me to bed. I fell asleep as soon as my head touched the pillow.

Mrs. Roemer knocked on my door at seven as she usually did, but I slept through it. I awoke at half past ten with a horrible headache. I went to put on my dress, but as soon as I smelled the odor of brandy on it, I immediately got sick. I washed it and washed it, but it was weeks before I could wear that dress again. Even six months later, when Mrs. Roemer used brandy in a recipe, I had to run to the bathroom as soon as she uncorked the bottle. As a matter of fact even to this day I can't tolerate the smell of brandy.

Scenes from the Hurricane's Eye

As Mrs. Roemer's time drew closer, a steady stream of visitors arrived from Germany. The first was Fräulein Maria, a short, stout, extremely severe old maid, who came to arrange the nursery. Fräulein Maria was Mrs. Roemer's old nanny, the real boss of her parents' house in Dresden. Everyone in that family was a little afraid of her. According to Mrs. Roemer, she was a fanatical Nazi who got down on her knees at night and prayed to the picture of Hitler over her bed the way most people pray to Jesus. During the book-burning campaigns of the thirties, Mrs. Roemer's father had to hide his treasured volumes of Heine and Thomas Mann to save them from the fire. Needless to say, I did whatever Fräulein Maria told me to do exactly as she told me to do it, and we got along as well as might be expected.

Mrs. Roemer's parents arrived shortly afterward. They were an extremely refined and charming couple. I liked them very much, especially since Mrs. Roemer's father behaved himself. Before they arrived, Mrs. Roemer warned me that her father liked to smack women on the behind. No one in the family was immune, not even Fräulein Maria! I shuddered at the thought of anyone doing that to me. I begged Mrs. Roemer to write to her father and ask him to control himself during his stay. She did. She wrote her father a long letter explaining that Fräulein Wanda *hates* to be smacked on the behind and that he *must* be very, very careful to restrain himself. I must say that he behaved like a perfect gentleman.

The baby was born at the end of December, just before New Year's Eve. It was a very difficult birth, and, as a result of complications during delivery, little Klaus was born with a club foot. Mrs. Roemer was heartbroken, and

Colonel Roemer was mortified at the thought of his son being a cripple. However, the staff doctor, a Viennese specialist, assured them that the damage need not be permanent. Before we brought the baby home from the hospital, he showed us how to massage the little foot and wrap it a special way in an elastic bandage. He also taught us a series of gymnastic exercises to practice with Klaus to help him develop his leg muscles. According to the doctor, if we maintained the daily program of massage and exercise, Klaus's foot would straighten out and he would be walking normally by the time he was three. Mrs. Roemer watched carefully the first few times I practiced the routine to make sure I was doing it correctly. Once she saw that I knew what to do, she stopped worrying. I had complete charge of that baby.

Complete charge meant exactly that. Mrs. Roemer was recovering from the birth and was in no condition to care for an infant. I bathed him, rocked him, fed him. I changed his diapers, massaged his foot, and sang him lullabies to soothe his sleep. When he woke up crying in the middle of the night, I was the one who rushed to his crib. He was a beautiful, happy baby who loved his Fräulein Wanda as much as I loved him.

Now that the baby had arrived, Colonel Roemer decided he was entitled to another servant. He knew just the man: an SS private from Alsace named Karl-Heinz who worked as a restaurant cook and pastry chef in civilian life. As soon as Colonel Roemer found that Karl-Heinz had that professional training, he snatched him out of the ranks and made him his valet. In addition to doing our cooking, Karl-Heinz pressed Colonel Roemer's uniforms, polished his boots, ran his errands, and generally acted like the flunky he was. Every time the colonel turned around, there was Karl-Heinz saluting, clicking his heels, shouting, "*Jawohl, Herr Kommandant!*"

I never had much use for people like Karl-Heinz, but I must admit that he was an excellent cook. Every meal was like a dinner in a fine restaurant. If the path to the Kommandant's heart was through his stomach, Karl-Heinz was well along the way.

Karl-Heinz also did special jobs for Colonel Roemer. Someone gave the colonel a dog, a pedigreed fox terrier. Colonel Roemer got a special pass for me so I could walk it on the street after curfew. It was a nice little dog, but one day it committed an unpardonable sin. It ate the dinner roast; and a dinner to which Colonel Roemer's commanding officer was invited. The colonel was furious. He told Karl-Heinz to take the dog out the next day and sell him. Karl-Heinz sold him to a Pole for two thousand zlotys. But the dog apparently didn't like its new home because a few days later it ran away and came back.

"What is the dog doing here?" I asked Karl-Heinz when I came back from shopping and found the dog sitting in the kitchen.

"He came back."

"But aren't you going to return him to the man who bought him?"

"What for? Who brings back dogs?"

So Colonel Roemer kept his dog and pocketed two thousand zlotys. So much for German morality.

Two months after Klaus came home, Mrs. Roemer asked my help in preparing a big dinner. Colonel Roemer was being considered for promotion. A general was coming down from Berlin and a great deal depended on his recommendation. Mrs. Roemer gave me her shopping list, and off

I went to the black market. That was one important advantage the Germans in Poland had over their compatriots in Germany. The black market was tolerated in Poland. In Germany it wasn't. I never took money with me when I went shopping. I didn't have to. A bottle of vodka and a few cartons of cigarettes were more than enough to buy a dozen eggs, a chicken, or whatever else we needed even when the shelves in the official stores were bare. This time I came back with my arms full. Karl-Heinz set to work and outdid himself. What a superb dinner that was! There was a rabbit braten with ham, a goose stuffed with liver and apples, and all sorts of wonderful pastries for dessert. Everything was cooked to perfection. Colonel Roemer was glowing. The general declared it the best meal he ever had. Later, over brandy and cigars, he assured Colonel Roemer that the promotion was his . . . except for one small detail. He had to have another son.

A few days after our glorious dinner I found Mrs. Roemer crying in her bedroom. I asked what was wrong, and she told me. Because of what she had gone through giving birth to Klaus, the doctor warned her not to even think of having another child for at least a year. But as soon as Colonel Roemer learned his promotion depended on it, he made up his mind to get her pregnant again as soon as possible. When it came to his career, not even his wife's health—not even her life—was allowed to stand in his way.

Colonel Roemer had detailed plans for his family's future as well as my own. After the war—which the Germans were naturally going to win—he was going to buy a large estate in Austria. In fact, he already had one manor in mind. And, of course, I was going with him to take care of the house and supervise the upbringing of little Klaus and all the other little Roemer children he had planned. I was going to be another Fräulein Maria but on a much grander scale, with a whole staff of nannies and maids working under me. However, I needed a husband, preferably someone who could manage the grounds while I looked after the household. Colonel Roemer knew of an SS sergeant in Prague who would be perfect. There was only one problem. The elite SS were forbidden to marry "subhuman" Poles. But, according to Colonel Roemer, I was obviously no ordinary Pole. I had character and intelligence, the very qualities to make me the perfect wife for an SS man. Could that be an accident? No. I could not possibly be a pure Slav. Superior Aryan blood must lie somewhere in my family tree. Colonel Roemer made an appointment for me to undergo a complete racial examination. Experts carefully measured my head, thighs, arms, and face and came to the conclusion that I definitely had a Nordic skull.

"You see! I was right all along!" Colonel Roemer crowed when he read the examination report. "When this war is over, we'll make an official Aryan out of you. You'll marry a fine SS man, and we'll all live together on my estate in Austria. I'll invite all the big shots in the Reich up for hunting, and in the evenings we'll have gala parties. Do you realize how lucky you are, Wanda? What better future could you have than this?"

What could I say to that?

By spring Mrs. Roemer was looking forward to going out again. She asked her parents to send all her spring outfits to Kraków. But her pregnancy had altered her figure slightly, and many of her dresses had to be let out. She took them to a tailor shop in the ghetto, where the last surviving Jews in the city clung to life by doing alterations for SS officers and their families. I accompanied Mrs. Roemer for the final fittings, and my heart broke to see how few and how desperately frightened my fellow Jews were. But I didn't dare show my feelings.

On our way home Mrs. Roemer asked if I had a spring outfit. When I admitted I didn't, she said, "Why don't you find a secondhand man's suit and have it altered. A good tailor could make it into a lovely jacket and skirt." That was an excellent idea because fashionable women's skirts were narrow and the jackets that went with them were very similar to men's. The next time I did the wash for Adrian, I asked if he knew where I could buy a man's suit. As it happened, he had an old one he was willing to sell: a dark gray suit flecked with red, with a tiny silver pinstripe running through it. I bought it and took it to the tailor at the barracks, who altered it. I looked and felt terrific in that suit. No more hiding in the nursery for me! Winter was over. Now it was spring, and I was eager to see the world outside.

Mrs. Roemer was so taken with how I looked in my new suit that she insisted on my borrowing her leather gloves and silk stockings on Sunday, when I took the morning off to go to church. But I never went to church. Instead I went to the concerts held every Sunday at a nearby movie house. I first learned of the series through an advertisement in the *Krakauer Zeitung*, the local German newspaper. A different choral group or orchestra was featured every week. Some were local, others were on tour from Germany, but all were excellent. Nevertheless, I couldn't help but notice certain ironies. On one occasion an orchestra played Beethoven's Ninth Symphony while onstage a military chorus of soldiers, SS, and nurses sang the glorious words *"Alle Menschen werden Brüder . . ."*

Scenes from the Hurricane's Eye

"Well, well," I thought as I listened, "look who's singing about the brotherhood of man. So all men are brothers, are they? All men . . . but not the Jews."

One afternoon Mrs. Roemer asked if I would like to go to the theater to see a performance of *Faust*. I knew which performance she was talking about. The advertisements were all over the newspaper. It was a first-rate German production playing in what had been the Polish National Theater, one of the most modern theaters in Europe and one of the first to be equipped with a revolving stage. Tickets were very expensive and restricted to Germans, so I hadn't even considered going until Mrs. Roemer mentioned it. She and her husband had two seats in the orchestra for the evening performance. However, an emergency came up, and they couldn't go. Mrs. Roemer, knowing how much I loved the theater, offered her ticket to me.

Reading a play in school and seeing it performed on the stage are two different experiences. The music, lighting, costumes, sets, and the exceptional acting made each word come alive. I never thought such magical effects possible, but there they were onstage before my eyes. At times I nearly leaped from my seat with excitement. Other times I was moved to tears. I didn't want the performance to end, but when the curtain finally closed I stood up and applauded until my palms ached.

The next day I told Mrs. Roemer all about the play. She was so thrilled that I enjoyed myself that she promised to get me tickets to other operas and operettas. I saw *Die Fledermaus*, *Der Rosenkavalier*, and all the masterpieces of the German stage. Every time there was a special performance in Kraków, there I was sitting in the reserved section with high officers and officials and their wives, savoring not only the delights of the theater but a personal triumph as well. "You stupid Germans," I thought to myself as I looked around at all the glittering uniforms. "I'm supposed to be dead, but I'm not. On this gala evening I'm sitting right beside you in this reserved section watching this special performance. And in spite of all your charts and measurements and elaborate racial theories, not a single one of you can tell I'm Jewish. To hell with you, then, and to hell with your arrogant 'Master Race' nonsense!"

As the weather grew warmer, I began taking Klaus outside more often. After clearing away the breakfast dishes, I cooked his formula, fed him, gave him a bath, got him dressed, put him in the buggy, and out we went for a stroll.

The apartment where we lived was on Bernardinska Street, on the same block as the barracks and the Bernardine church, a famous Kraków landmark. Before the war the Bernardine fathers maintained the whole complex, with a school, a large private garden, and a residence for priests. In 1939 the SS evicted the Bernardines and took over the facility, turning it into the headquarters where I worked. The commissary acquired the garden, dug up most of the flower beds, and used the space to grow vegetables. A few rows of fruit trees remained standing. It had been an elegant garden once, and the rosebushes and flower beds that remained were carefully tended.

Every morning, weather permitting, I would take Klaus to that garden. There we would sit for an hour or so, catching the sun. Sometimes, if I felt restless, I would lay the baby down on the grass nearby while I talked with the gardener or the two soldiers who were always on guard. Sometimes I even helped with the weeding. Other times

I would crochet or read while Klaus napped. Time passed very quickly.

Safe, protected from the prying eyes of suspicious strangers, I began to feel like a human being once more and not like a hunted animal. As a result of my new-found security, I began to read again after more than a year. I went to the main library in Kraków whenever I had free time. One day I took home a copy of *Gone with the Wind.* I started the book one spring day as I was sitting with Klaus in the garden. After having read a few pages I became so absorbed in the story that it was well into the afternoon before I realized it was time to go home. For the whole next week I spent every spare moment reading until I came to the end. I was never so moved by a book before. It totally changed my way of thinking.

Before that, I had been living in a dream world. I believed that one day the war would be over, my family would return, and life would continue happily as before. After reading Scarlett O'Hara's story, I realized I was fooling myself. The Piotrków of my childhood was gone. Never again would I walk those familiar streets, stopping by the shops and courtyards to visit my friends and say hello to people I knew. That world was gone forever.

"You forgot," I told myself, "it all happened before. In America, the South was destroyed. A whole way of life vanished. Even after the war, when Scarlett went home to Tara, it wasn't the same—and it would never be the same again." When I came to the part where Scarlett reads the names of her friends who died in battle, for me the list read "Gershon . . . Shimon . . . Moshe." I took the mask off my heart. I had played a false role so long I forgot who I really was. Now I was Ruszka Guterman again. Or rather I was Scarlett O'Hara. Like her, I had no doubt about my own survival. But the friends I remembered, the people I loved, were never going to return. There simply was no going back. I had avoided that fact for a long time. Now I had to face it. As I turned the last page of the book I thought, "It was the end of a southern culture. It is the end of a Jewish culture. And no matter what the future may bring, it will never bring back the past."

That realization, more than any of the terrors I experienced, plunged me into a deep depression. "Why go on?" I thought to myself. "Even if the Germans are defeated some day, I will never go back to Judaism. Never! I have suffered too much. And for what? Now that I have my new identity and a complete set of papers, I will carry my secret to the grave. No one will ever know that I am Jewish. I will never run like a hunted animal again. When the war is over I will marry a Polish man and raise Polish children—one-hundred-percent Polish children!—who will never have to suffer the persecution Jews have to endure."

That was my lowest point, and it shames me to think I actually considered betraying all my father's hopes and the sole reason for my survival. Yet these thoughts passed through my mind. Then, when my spirits needed it most, I received a tremendous boost.

Once a week Colonel and Mrs. Roemer went out for the evening. After putting Klaus to bed, I usually sat down in the living room and listened to the radio. I had my own little radio in Klaus's room which I listened to while ironing his diapers or taking care of other chores, but the radio in the living room was a big shortwave console that could pick up stations all over the world.

One evening I started turning the dial to see what I could pick up when all of a sudden the words *"Mówi Moskwa, Mówi Moskwa, Mówi Moskwa"* came over the speaker. It was Radio Moscow broadcasting in Polish. I made a note of the channel, and after that, whenever the Roemers went out, I went straight to the radio and tuned in. Before long I was also listening to the BBC broadcasts in Polish and German. The news that I got from the Allied stations was quite different from what I read in the German press. According to the *Krakauer Zeitung*, the war was going splendidly. The Allies were in full retreat and the German Army totally victorious everywhere, except that minor adjustments had to be made every now and then to "straighten out the lines." One evening over the radio I heard about a big "straightening out" at a place called Stalingrad. General Paulus and the entire German Sixth Army had surrendered to the Russians in a stunning defeat. Hundreds of thousands of German soldiers were prisoners. I sat glued to the radio, trying to hear every detail. I was ecstatic! This was the first major setback for the Germans, the first crack in their armor. I knew that final victory for the Allies was coming. "Soon," I kept telling myself, "soon it will be over."

I was so excited about the news that I nearly gave myself away. Some days later Mrs. Roemer happened to mention something about the eastern front. "Oh, yes," I replied. "Isn't it terrible about Stalingrad and General Paulus."

Mrs. Roemer looked at me, quite surprised. "Fräulein Wanda, how do you know?"

I covered up quickly. "I read about it in the *Kraukauer Zeitung*."

But the story wasn't in the *Kraukauer Zeitung*, which still only talked about "straightening out the lines." In the future I would have to be more careful about revealing what I knew to Mrs. Roemer and other Germans. But whenever I went down to the barracks I told my friends

Mr. Zak and Stasiek the janitor everything. Since I listened to the broadcasts regularly, I quickly became an authority on the world situation. "If Wanda says so, it must be true," they used to say.

But the news wasn't always good. One evening, knowing that the Roemers would be home shortly. I tuned to the local German station in time to catch a news broadcast. All the ghetto camps in Poland were to be closed down and the inmates "resettled." I shivered to hear that word. Every Jew knew what it really meant. The announcer then read a list of cities: "Krakau . . . Pieterkau . . ." *Piotrków!* That single word snapped me back to another existence, a world of pain and terror. Faces came into my mind—Mayer's, Renia's, my father's—all the people I knew who were still alive somewhere, somehow, in the ghetto. What would become of them now? Before me flashed the black uniforms, the snarling dogs, the whips. I saw the cattle cars waiting at the sidings, the barbed wire stretched across the sky, the smoke billowing from the blackened chimneys. Seething rage and despair swept over me as I reached out to turn off the radio. I stood alone in the elegantly furnished living room, trembling.

Then I heard a cry—a tiny, choked wail. It was Klaus crying in the nursery. He had awakened in the dark and, frightened, cried for his Fräulein Wanda. But it wasn't his Fräulein Wanda who hurried to his side. It was an automaton driven by a cold, passionless fury. I picked Klaus up as I had done a hundred times before and started giving him his bottle. He soon quieted down. I took the bottle away and set it on the nursery table and stood there holding him. Then slowly, steadily, I began to squeeze. Yes. Squeeze him. Squeeze the life out of him, just as they squeezed the life out of my little sister, out of my parents and friends, out of all the little children they beat or shot or gassed or starved to death. Let them know what it feels like to hold a dead child in their arms.

Klaus looked up. He didn't understand. His Wanda, his dear Fräulein Wanda, who fed and bathed and always took care of him, was hurting him. He began to cry.

That baby's cry snapped me back to my senses. Had I gone mad? What was I doing? He was only a baby, an innocent baby who loved and trusted me. How could I do him harm?

"There, there." I soothed Klaus to stop his crying. I gave him his bottle once more and in a little while he went back to sleep. But it was a long time before I stopped trembling.

The End
in Sight

After Stalingrad the tide slowly shifted. Battles raged along the eastern front, but this time it was the Russians who attacked. By 1944 the German Army was in retreat. The Red Army entered eastern Poland in July. By August they held Lublin and were advancing on Warsaw. The front was crumbling.

Colonel Roemer's faith in a German victory, however, remained unshaken. These were only temporary setbacks, he insisted. The Germans were preparing a vast counterattack. When it was launched, the Soviets would be annihilated. However—purely as a precautionary measure—he decided to send Klaus and Mrs. Roemer back to Germany. A few days later the Mercedes was loaded, and, with the chauffeur at the wheel, the Roemers and I drove west.

It was a pleasant ride through the countryside. We passed towns and fields. Horses and cattle grazed in open pastures. After an hour we passed a road sign: "Auschwitz—10 KM." I felt as if an icicle had been driven through my heart. That dreadful name! That awful place! It was only a small distance away. Even now as I rode through this tranquil countryside in this chauffeur-driven limousine, making small talk with an SS colonel and his wife, holding their sleeping baby in my arms, thousands of Jews—my family and friends perhaps among them—were choking out their lives in ovens and gas chambers. Were it not for a few accidents of fate, I might well be with them, reading that same sign through the cracks in the door of a cattle car. How hard it was, wearing my mask, pretending that Auschwitz meant no more to me than the name of any country hamlet. I did it then because my life depended on it. But even now I can close my eyes and still see that sign.

In a little while we came to the border. The guards at the checkpoint looked at the Mercedes, saluted Colonel Roemer, and waved us through. No one asked to see my papers. For all the attention paid to me, I might have been one of the suitcases. We drove on to Katowice, where we stopped for lunch at the rathskeller. Afterward we continued to the railway station and put Mrs. Roemer and Klaus on the next train for Magdeburg. Mrs. Roemer gave me a quick good-bye. She didn't intend to be gone long—only a few weeks, until the danger at the front had passed. But before she left, she made her husband promise to take care of me. Colonel Roemer swore he would. However, he didn't always keep his promises.

Once Mrs. Roemer and Klaus were gone, my role in the household was much less important than it had been. Before I was a nanny; now I was a maid. Karl-Heinz started giving me orders. He never had any authority over me before. Since when did I take orders from him? I protested, but Colonel Roemer backed Karl-Heinz, who, as his power increased, began finding new ways to harass me.

My new taskmaster had a whole schedule worked out. "Pay attention, Wanda," he said. "I am going to tell you what you have to do. First, you are going to wash all the kitchen tiles. I want the oven cleaned, too, as well as the walls and ceiling. When Mrs. Roemer comes back, I want her to find this place spick-and-span. You are not going to sit here and do nothing. Now, how much time will it take you to wash this wall?"

I couldn't believe he was serious. "Karl-Heinz, what are you talking about? If you want the wall washed, I'll wash it. When it's done, it's done."

"Oh, no! We are not going to work like that. That's the Polish way of doing things. From now on we are going to get organized. I have to know how much time these tasks are going to take because I am going to write it all down. That way I can report to Colonel Roemer whether or not you're on schedule. Let's see. Two hours, walls. Twenty minutes, dishes . . ."

He went out of his way to hound me. There was no escaping him. He was on my back all day. If I stopped for a moment to catch my breath, there he was—"I am going to tell Colonel Roemer you are lazy! I am going to tell Colonel Roemer you are rebellious!"

One day he pushed me too far. I had just finished cleaning the baking oven. Karl-Heinz decided to inspect my work. That little skunk even stuck his head up the chimney to see if I had cleaned out the soot! This was the last straw. "The devil with you, Karl-Heinz!" I shouted. "I don't have to take this! I'm not your slave! I can go to Colonel Roemer, too. As for you, you can go to hell!"

"Go ahead," he sneered. "And while you're talking to Colonel Roemer, why don't you also tell him how you managed to skip out of the ghetto?"

It was just like him to say that; to hint that I was Jewish. That was the rumor about me. It was all over the barracks. There was nothing to do but throw the accusation back in his face.

"And you, Karl-Heinz, are the biggest apple polisher that ever lived!"

Oh, how he made my life miserable after that! He wrote out a complete schedule for every day of the week. He had me climbing up and down ladders as I raced to finish walls, windows, ceilings. If I fell behind, there he was, complaining, making threats. If I finished ahead of schedule, he found something else for me to do. I didn't have a minute to myself. I protested to Colonel Roemer, but he backed Karl-Heinz completely. What could I do? I had no choice but to obey. But I made sure Karl-Heinz knew I wasn't afraid of him. Whenever he began threatening me, I threatened him right back. "Just you wait, Karl-Heinz. You wait till Mrs. Roemer gets back. Then it's going to be your turn!"

One day the doorsill to one of the rooms worked loose. Karl-Heinz went out to get someone to fix it. In a little while he came back with a sad-looking man in a blue-and-white–striped concentration-camp uniform. The man's head was shaved, and although I did not speak to him, I was sure he was Jewish, especially when Karl-Heinz laughed, "Hey, Wanda! Look here! I brought you a boyfriend!"

During this period the only time I was alone was in the evening. Karl-Heinz returned to the barracks after dinner. Colonel Roemer spent most of his time at his private apartment at the barracks. I might not see him for days. He came and went as he pleased, never troubling to let his servants know when he might be coming home. Nevertheless, whenever he came through that door—day or night—he expected me to be on duty, ready to wait on him.

One evening, when I was sound asleep, I was awakened by a knocking at my bedroom door.

"Fräulein Wanda, get up. Please come and make coffee."

I looked at my watch. It was two o'clock in the morning! Colonel Roemer and several of his officers were having a meeting in the living room. He wanted me to serve refreshments. I threw on my clothes, went to the kitchen, got the coffee ready, arranged the little cups on the coffee table, and began serving. Glancing up, I noticed Colonel Roemer staring at me. He looked very displeased.

"Fräulein Wanda," he finally said, "you haven't made yourself presentable. Your hair isn't combed. You don't look neat."

What nerve! He comes home without warning in the dead of night, wakes me up, demands I serve coffee immediately, then stands back and criticizes because I don't look presentable. His wife might put up with that behavior, but not I. "I'm here to pour the coffee," I snapped, "not to make a good impression."

That was the way I talked to Colonel Roemer whenever he started his bullying, but I went too far this time. I

The End in Sight

181

had embarrassed him in front of his officers—not a wise thing to do, especially now that Mrs. Roemer was no longer there to defend me. Nothing came of that incident, but it probably set the stage for a more serious one that took place sometime later.

Soon after Mrs. Roemer went back to Germany, the authorities started evacuating not only German nationals but ethnic Germans as well. Two of our neighbors, a widow and her son—both ethnic Germans—received orders to pack up and prepare for evacuation to Germany. The widow was a pleasant person who, unlike most of the other ethnic Germans, tried to maintain good relations with her Polish neighbors. Everyone saw the departure of the ethnic Germans as simply one more sign that victory was on the way, but we didn't bear our neighbor any grudge and hoped that all would be well with her. The night before she left, all the Poles living in the building gathered in the janitor's apartment for a farewell party. The widow was touched. She told us she had no idea where she was going, but would write as soon as she had a permanent address. We talked about the political situation and other matters. By the time I looked at my watch, it was nearly twelve o'clock.

I ran upstairs to the Roemers' apartment and tried to unlock the door with my key. It wouldn't open. Someone inside had slipped on the chain lock. I was fumbling with the door, trying to loosen the chain, when Colonel Roemer appeared.

"Where have you been?" he shouted. "You're not paid to run around all night! You're paid to stay here in the house!"

"Colonel Roemer," I tried to explain. "I wasn't running around. I was downstairs. We were having a little party for the widow. She's leaving tomorrow for Germany.

Ask the others downstairs if you don't believe me. They'll tell you where I was."

He refused to listen. "Wherever you were, you can turn around and go back. I'm not letting you in. Tomorrow morning you will report to my office." He slammed the door in my face.

To hell with him! I wasn't going to sleep in the street just to please Colonel Roemer. I remembered that the windows on the staircase overlooked the apartment balconies. I ran upstairs to the next landing, opened the window, climbed through, and dropped down onto the balcony below. The building's balconies were continuous. I walked along outside until I came to the Roemers' apartment. The kitchen door was always unlocked. I opened it, slipped through, tiptoed to my bedroom, and hopped into bed.

The next morning I reported to Colonel Roemer's office at the barracks. Without a word to me he summoned two soldiers, marched me downstairs to the basement jail, and locked me up in one of the cells. "I hope this does you some good," he said before leaving. "Since you obviously don't appreciate good treatment, you can just sit!"

I sat for three days in that cell, not knowing what was going to happen to me. Finally Colonel Roemer decided I had learned my lesson. He ordered my release and had me brought back to the apartment. He was waiting for me. First he demanded to know how I got back in that night. I started to tell him, but he cut me off. "No. You are not going to tell me. You are going to show me." In order to satisfy him, I was forced to go upstairs to the landing and demonstrate exactly how I climbed through the window, jumped down onto the balcony, and came in through the kitchen.

After I came in, Colonel Roemer told me that Karl-

Heinz was in charge. I was to obey him and do whatever he said. Furthermore, it was my job to remain in the house and keep an eye on things. I was to be there every night after curfew . . . or else! What choice did I have? He dismissed me, and everything continued as before. Nevertheless, the whole episode left me sick at heart. Even though I had gotten off fairly easily, I could never forget that my life hung suspended by a very slender thread. A glittering sword, poised to cut it off, was never far away.

In August an uprising broke out in Warsaw. The next few days were extremely tense. We expected the Russians to take advantage of the situation and cross the Vistula. But they made no move. They were content to look on while the Germans handled the job of crushing the Polish nationalists. Whatever hopes of liberation I had were premature. By October the uprising was extinguished. Warsaw was still in German hands, and the Russians were still on the other side of the Vistula with no sign of advancing soon. There was nothing to do but wait.

Then one day Colonel Roemer told me to fix up the nursery and buy some flowers to decorate the apartment. Mrs. Roemer and Klaus were coming home. I was overjoyed.

After Mrs. Roemer's return, Karl-Heinz went back to his role as the Kommandant's valet while I resumed my duties in the nursery. I didn't say anything about my treatment to Mrs. Roemer at first. I was not even sure I wanted to discuss it with her. But after a few days she asked me how I had gotten along while she was gone. That was when I told her everything. She became quite upset, especially when she heard about my three nights in jail. She could not understand treating a trusted family servant in that manner.

But that was the difference between Mrs. Roemer and her husband. He felt no loyalty, no obligation to anyone but himself, as Karl-Heinz was soon to learn. Constant calls for more men came from the front. Finally the day came when Colonel Roemer decided he could live without a cook, and off Karl-Heinz went to the Russian front.

With Karl-Heinz gone, life quickly settled back into its normal routine. I bathed Klaus, fed him, changed his diapers, and took him for walks. The Roemers went out to dinner several nights a week, and usually the wives of other SS officers came over in the afternoon for coffee. Colonel Roemer and I were getting along again. He seemed to enjoy the fact that I refused to cringe before him, although he threw me in jail for that very reason only a few weeks before.

One Sunday afternoon a young officer from Vienna was invited over for coffee. I answered the door when the bell rang. The poor fellow, taking me for the lady of the house, bowed low, took my hand, and with a great flourish addressed me as "gnädige Frau . . . gracious lady." Colonel Roemer stepped into the hallway and saw the whole performance. Only when the officer finished his elaborate salutation did he finally say, "Fräulein Wanda, will you please call my wife?" The poor man was mortified. I felt sorry for him, but it was hard to keep from laughing. Colonel Roemer teased me about it for months. "Gnädige Fräulein Wanda," he'd chuckle, "would you be so kind as to clear away these dishes?"

The pleasantries of our daily life could not cover up the fact that the military situation was becoming more ominous by the day. The *Krakauer Zeitung* still insisted that the German Army was only "straightening out the lines." I sat glued to the radio every time the Roemers went out, so I knew better.

As for the general population, its first tangible sign of how bad the situation really was came when trainloads of Polish civilians were taken from their jobs to the outskirts of Kraków to dig trenches. Initially I was exempt. But when our turn came, everyone in the barracks, from the waitress in the officers' canteen to the potato scrubbers in the kitchen, had to go. Eventually the day came when Colonel Roemer said to me, "Wanda, you must do your duty the same as all the other Poles. The next time our civilian workers are scheduled to go, you're going, too."

And I did go. There were six in our group: the battalion tailor; his niece who assisted him in the shop; her boyfriend the commissary clerk; a washerwoman; the man who took care of the boilers; and me. We all had very mixed feelings about the trip. On the one hand we were hardly looking forward to digging trenches in the dead of winter, but on the other this was the first real sign that our liberation might be near.

The train took us to the stone quarries at the edge of the city. From there we rode in wagons to the trenches. The excursion quickly became like a holiday outing. Soon we were all joking and singing. To hell with the Germans! If they had to dig tank traps this close to Kraków, it was a sure sign that the Russians weren't far away.

When we arrived at the trenches, we were given shovels and told what to do. These trenches were a two-step affair. One person dug on the lower tier, a second on the upper. The trenches were deep. We had to throw the sand up high. The only Germans in sight were a guard and the engineer supervising the project. He told us to work hard and that all talking was forbidden.

It was bitter cold. Frost covered the ground. Our breath came out in great white clouds. In the nearby field we could see a peasant's hut. Smoke was coming out of the chimney, a sign that a warm fire was burning inside in the stove. I was assigned to dig with the tailor, his niece, and her boyfriend. No matter how hard I worked, I was still freezing. So were the others. After a short while the tailor's niece put down her shovel. "Come on, Wanda," she said. "Let's sneak over to that hut. We'll get warm and have a little drink." As soon as the guard turned his back, that's what we all did. As we huddled around the stove trying to drive the chill from our bones, the boyfriend took a bottle of vodka and a six-ounce glass out of his coat. He filled the glass to the brim and handed it to me.

"You don't seriously expect me to drink all that, do you?" I asked him.

"Of course!" he insisted.

So I did. Suddenly I began to feel very warm. In fact, I felt so good I had another glass. All in all I believe I drank eight ounces of straight vodka before we went back to work. By the time I got back to those frozen trenches I fully appreciated the merits of alcohol.

If the Germans expected to get much work out of us, they were badly mistaken. The toilet was at the far end of the field. The tailor's niece and I asked the guard for permission to go. What could he say? It was a long walk there and a long walk back. We didn't hurry, and while we were there, we sat for a good long time. That killed at least half an hour, and we did it a couple of times. At ten o'clock the whole platoon broke off work to get something to eat. By

The End in Sight

noon everyone was frozen, even the Germans, so we all ran to the hut to get warm. No one made the least pretense of doing anything further. We were jubilant. In spite of the cold everyone was laughing and singing. The Germans were in big trouble! How could the holes they had us digging stop a tank? They were barely a yard wide, and certainly no one was working very hard to finish them. But what did we care? Maybe the Germans wanted those Russian tanks stopped, but as far as we were concerned, the tanks couldn't get here fast enough.

Long after dark, when I finally came home. Mrs. Roemer had dinner waiting on the table for me and hot water drawn for a bath.

Although I went to dig trenches on several other occasions, I failed to see how any of those defenses had grown more effective since the first time I was there. It was going to take more than a few holes in the ground to stop the Russians when they attacked. The Poles could see it. I'm certain the Germans saw it, too. Back in the barracks an air of unconcerned calm prevailed. But as we drifted into the Christmas season, cracks in the façade began to appear. I noticed faces looking east. It was obvious what people were thinking. The Russians would not remain on the Vistula forever. The river was icing up. Before long they would be on the move. And then?

The Poles had been expressing these thoughts for months. Now for the first time I began hearing them from Germans. The first was Nikischer, who managed the barracks canteen. I got to know him well as a result of my frequent errands there for Colonel Roemer. Once we became friendly, Nikischer let me know when special shipments came in. He let me buy many things for myself: cigarettes, cigarette papers, tobacco, perfume, cookies, and other luxury items I could resell on the black market for considerable profit. Nikischer was an interesting character with an international background. His parents had emigrated to America when he was a boy, taking his younger brother with them but leaving him behind to be raised in Germany by his grandparents. He saw his brother in 1939, just before the war, when he came over for a visit. The brother was now a sergeant in the American army. Nikischer was married to a Dutch woman he had met while he was stationed in the Netherlands. I always dropped by his office whenever I went to the canteen. He used to say, "With a Dutch wife and an American brother, don't you think I'm a prime candidate for the other side?" He always said it teasingly, but lately I noticed he was saying it more often. Then he told me about a dream he once had.

"I dreamed I was in Italy or somewhere else on the western front. I was on the line, shooting my rifle, when I looked over on the other side, and there was my brother. I saw him waving to me. I heard him call, 'Come on over! Come on! Come on!' So I threw my rifle away, put up my hands, and walked over to him." He laughed, as if it were all a joke. But SS men don't make jokes like that— unless they are seriously demoralized.

Later on I heard about a soldier in the barracks who was actually arrested for making defeatist remarks. But the most telling sign of all came when Mrs. Roemer's younger brother was called up for military service. Instead of waiting to be drafted into the army, he wanted to volunteer for the SS. His parents were against it, but the boy was determined. The person who ultimately dissuaded him was Colonel

Roemer. "Don't do it," he advised the lad. "You'll only spoil things with the old folks."

When I heard that story from Mrs. Roemer, I knew the end must be near. For Colonel Roemer, the ultimate SS man, to talk his brother-in-law out of joining meant that even he no longer believed a German victory was possible. The end was so close I felt I could reach out and touch it.

Into the Camp

All during this period, while I was with the Roemers, I received letters from Piotrków. They came by way of a friend of Renia's, a Polish girl named Krysia, whose family had a small farm on the outskirts of the city. My father and Mayer passed their letters to Renia, who took them with her to her job in the tailoring shop outside the ghetto. Krysia dropped by every so often, picked up the letters, and mailed them. To send letters into the ghetto, the process worked in reverse. I addressed my letters to Krysia, who passed them to Renia, who delivered them to my father and Mayer. Thus I was able to maintain contact the whole time I was in Kraków.

For months I searched for a place for my father. I was determined to get him out of the ghetto. But that by itself was not the problem. The real question was what he would do once he was out. It wasn't enough merely to slip over the wall. That was just the beginning. A Jew on the run needed money. He needed a job. He needed a whole collection of papers: baptismal certificate, identity card, work card, ration card, residence permit. Most important, he had to get away from the Polish populace, whose members delighted in the sport of sniffing out runaway Jews. I knew my father could survive if I could only find the right place for him. But where? As a cleaning woman or kitchen worker, my contacts were few. His only place would have been with me, and I knew he would never agree to that. It was too dangerous. In the meantime I purchased an excellent set of false papers and sent them to him. Then I waited.

Once I started working for the Roemers, the situation changed. With all my contacts through Mrs. Roemer and the barracks, something was sure to turn up. And it did. One day I learned of a job opening in Zakopane running a hostel for wounded soldiers. It was a perfect job for my father. He would be out in the countryside, dealing exclusively with Germans instead of Poles. Should anyone ask questions, he could easily pass himself off as a Ukrainian. With Mrs. Roemer's help and Colonel Roemer's influence, I knew I could get my father that job. But first I had to get him out of the ghetto.

Some free time was due me, so I asked Mrs. Roemer for a few days off and took the train to Piotrków. It was early July, 1944, and the brilliant summer sun shone down on a countryside dappled with wheat fields and sunflowers. When I reached the city, I went directly to Krysia's house. Her mother let me in.

"I'm Wanda Gajda, a friend of your daughter's," I said, introducing myself.

The woman greeted me warmly. She knew who I was because my name was on the return address of the letters Krysia received from Kraków. I have no idea if she suspected I was Jewish or realized the extent to which her daughter was involved in the underground movement. In any case she was extremely hospitable. She asked if I had a place to stay and, when I admitted I didn't, insisted I stay with them. The summer vegetables were just coming in, and food was plentiful.

When Krysia came home, her mother told her her friend Wanda had arrived from Kraków. We greeted each other like two old friends though we had never seen each other before. It wasn't until after dinner that we had a chance to talk.

"What brings you to Piotrków?" Krysia asked. She knew I wasn't just visiting.

"I want to make contact with Renia. I have to get into the ghetto."

Krysia shook her head. "It's not going to be easy. They've closed the shop. Renia works in another place. There's a guard at the door. You can't just walk in. But we might have a chance to talk to her when she comes to work, Let's go down tomorrow morning and see."

We got up very early the next day and went down to the street opposite the main ghetto gate. We waited for several hours, but no one came out. It wasn't safe to wait anymore, so we went back. The next day we tried again, but the gates remained shut. No one went in or out. I couldn't wait any longer. I was due back in Kraków. So I left without seeing either Renia or my father. As it turned out, I never saw my father again.

I came so close, my heart aches to think of it. It was like reaching out to a drowning man and touching his fingers, only to have him slip from my grasp. Had I arrived a week or even a day earlier, my father could have lived.

The two days I waited outside the gate, the Germans were conducting a selection. They spared the young people to work in the glass and plywood factories. All the older workers, the sick, and the weak were trucked to the railway station, packed into boxcars, and shipped off to Auschwitz and its satellite camp, Blizin. Mayer was spared. So was Renia. But my father was taken to Blizin with the rest. He died there of typhoid fever. I didn't hear the full story until years later. When the Germans ordered all Jews out for the selection, my father vanished. He still had not given up—he still had the spirit to resist. But that collaborator, Holsztain, seeing him missing, took two soldiers, found his hiding place, and brought him back. Why did that scoundrel do it? Did he think he could save his own skin by betraying someone else? If that was his reason, it didn't work. The Germans didn't need him anymore. They shipped him off with the rest. But that betrayal was my father's death warrant. If he could have hidden until the selection was over, I could have come back and rescued him. I came so close.

I have one consolation. After the war, people who knew my father while he was in the camp told me how happy he was that my brother and I had gotten away and were doing well. He had no doubt that the war would end one day, that Hitler's gang would be destroyed, and that Benek and I would live to see it.

Though my father was gone, my correspondence with Mayer and Renia continued. I knew time was short. If I was going to do anything to save them, it would have to be soon. I racked my brain for possibilities, but there was none. The problem, as we all knew, was that they both looked Jewish. Mayer's case was hopeless. He knew he didn't stand a chance on the other side and bravely told me not to bother. Renia's problem was similar. She was short and plump with a dark complexion, but unlike Mayer she had a small nose and her features were subtler. She also had a gift for making friends and spoke impeccable Polish. A year or two before, that wouldn't have been enough, but it was 1944 and things had changed.

The German Army was retreating all along the Ukrainian front. As it pulled back, hordes of Russian and Ukrainian civilians followed. Most were simple refugees, but there were many collaborators among them.

Three women from this influx were assigned jobs at our barracks. One was a Polish Ukrainian from Lwów, the second, a Russian. According to the Russian woman's story, which she gladly related to anyone who cared to listen, she was married to a soldier in Vlasov's Army but didn't mind dating Germans while her husband was gone. When her boyfriends retreated, they took her along. The third claimed to be a Ukrainian. She had my old job peeling potatoes down in the basement.

The flotsam of eastern Europe was drifting through Kraków. Not only were people pouring in from the east, but after the Warsaw uprising of 1944, strangers began coming down from the north. Before, it was a sure bet that any rootless person was a Jew on the run. Now, one could not be that certain, and collaborators were so numerous that it wasn't even a good idea to ask questions. In such an environment Renia had a chance.

In November I heard the radio announcement that the last remnants of the Piotrków ghetto would be sent to

Auschwitz. If I ever hoped to do anything for Renia, I had to work fast.

I knew of one possibility. The battalion infirmary was around the corner from the barracks. It was always chronically short of nurses who were constantly being transferred to the front. I approached Colonel Roemer with an idea.

"I heard the infirmary lost its nurses again."

"That's right," he grumbled. "The last group was transferred out last week."

"I know of a girl in Piotrków who speaks German well and has studied nursing. She used to work in a hospital in Warsaw, so she has some practical experience, too. Since there's always such a shortage of nurses in the infirmary, don't you think it might be a good idea to hire her and train her for the job! I think she would work out well." I wasn't making this up. Everything I said was basically true. Renia did speak German and she used to work in the ghetto hospital.

Colonel Roemer thought it was a fine idea. The situation at the infirmary had been bothering him for some time. "Your friend will come work for us," he said. "We'll send her through the training course in Breslau, and when she's finished she'll come back here and be *our* nurse. Then, nobody can transfer her, and we won't have to put up with this constant turnover." He sent me over to the personnel officer to arrange for an immediate contract.

So far, so good. Now, if I could only get Renia out of the ghetto in time. I sent her a letter by way of Krysia outlining the situation. Once she arrived in Kraków, she would receive rations and be assigned a place to stay. Orientation would last a week. After that, she would go to Breslau for a special training course at the institute. I closed with the single word "Come!"

My letter arrived at the last possible moment, barely days before the ghetto's end. When Renia read that a job awaited her in Kraków, it was as if the door to life had opened up before her eyes. No matter what, she would find a way to come.

But the final liquidation came sooner than anyone anticipated. Hours before dawn, the last survivors were routed into the street, lined up, and marched to the trains. Renia managed to slip away as the group was being marched to the railway station, but an officer saw her. Two soldiers were sent to run her down and bring her back.

"Who helped you?" the officer demanded to know.

"No one. I ran away by myself."

Normally, Jews who tried to escape were shot, but this time the officer didn't bother. She would be dead soon enough anyway. He threw her back in line with the other women and marched the whole column down to the depot by the glass factory. There they were shoved into boxcars to await the next train. The Germans didn't bother to seal the cars. Where were those Jews going to go?

But Renia hadn't given up. She found herself standing next to a friend of ours, a young woman named Franka. She waited until the guards left. Then she said, "Franka, get ready. We're getting out of here."

"Where are we going?"

"To Kraków!"

They sneaked out the unlocked door on the opposite side of the car and made their way all across the city to Krysia's house. The family took them in and helped them formulate a plan of escape. The next morning they separated. Krysia's mother went with Renia while Krysia's older brother accompanied Franka. They went to the railway station and bought separate tickets. When the train arrived, they got on two separate cars. That was basic survival procedure in the underground: keep apart, stay separate. If one is caught, the other can still get away.

But Renia's luck ran out. The train was midway between Piotrków and Częstochowa when it was raided. Krysia's brother and Franka took off with the rest of the crowd, but Renia's car didn't get word in time. Before anyone realized what was happening, the police came through the door checking everyone's papers. They let Krysia's mother go, and while they didn't suspect Renia was Jewish (she had an excellent set of papers giving her name as Irena Zaporowska and listing a Warsaw address), they did arrest her for forced labor and marched her off with the others. She ended up in a camp outside of Częstochowa, where detainees were kept until they were shipped off to Germany.

I was awaiting Renia in Kraków when I received a frantic letter from her describing how she was arrested on the train and stuck in the camp. Could I get her out? That evening I spoke with Colonel Roemer. I told him that my friend Irena had been picked up on the train and was now sitting in a detention camp in Częstochowa waiting to be shipped out any day. It was really too bad, I added, because she was looking forward to taking the job in the infirmary and would have worked out well. Colonel Roemer was furious. Now he wasn't going to get his nurse. I showed him Renia's letter in which she mentioned a special release order that she had to have in order to be let out. Could the colonel help her obtain the proper papers?

The next morning Colonel Roemer ordered his secretary to draft a letter on official SS stationery declaring that Irena Zaporowska had a job as a nurse with the Third SS Pioneer Training Battalion and had qualified for the special course at the Nurses' Institute in Breslau. She was to be released immediately. It was a very impressive document.

But our problems weren't over. The Christmas season was rapidly approaching. All available trains were commandeered to take furloughed soldiers back to Germany. Even German civilians had to have special permission to travel. Poles couldn't travel by rail at all. Colonel Roemer had to obtain a special pass for me before I could even buy a ticket. This pass was also on SS stationery, was stamped, and had several official signatures at the bottom. It read: "Third SS Pioneer Training Battalion: The Pole, Wanda Gajda, has permission to travel on a Class A Express from Kraków to Częstochowa on December 27th and return on December 30th."

I packed my suitcase, bought my ticket, and took the first train out. It arrived in Częstochowa at ten-thirty, long after curfew. I was standing on the street as the train pulled out, wondering which way to go, when I saw a young woman go by. Her clothes were shabby and her head bowed as she shuffled slowly along the darkened street. She looked so lonely, so forlorn. I, in contrast, was wearing my best clothes: my gray coat with the fur collar, Mrs. Roemer's leather gloves, a black leather purse, and a stylish wine-red hat with shoes to match. No wonder she was surprised when I approached her and asked if she knew of a place where I could spend the night. Why should someone as well dressed as I bother talking to her at all?

"I have an apartment," she said shyly. "There's no one else there. You can come with me if you like."

I did. It was a bare garret room with a sleeping alcove and a tiny kitchen equipped with a potbellied stove. The place was freezing. We lit a fire to take off the chill. I offered her a box of cigarettes, but she refused. She wouldn't let me pay her at all. In fact, she acted as if I were doing her the favor instead of the other way around. I felt sorry for her. The poor woman was so lonely. She had no family, no friends, and here it was the Christmas season. She was thrilled to have company for even one night, even if it was only a stranger from the railway station. We talked for several hours before going to bed. She had to leave for work early, but she promised to leave the key under the doormat for me should I decide to stay another night.

I woke up early the next morning, but she was already gone. The woman had been very kind to me and I didn't want to take advantage of her, so just before leaving I left a pack of cigarettes on the table. Then I set out to find the camp.

It was located on the outskirts of Częstochowa, and I had to walk all the way there. I found the main office and asked for Renia. She wasn't available. All the detainees were out digging trenches and wouldn't be back until four. I saw no point in wasting the whole day, so I left a note for "Irena Zaporowska" saying that her friend Wanda Gajda had come to see her. Before leaving, I asked the clerk who had jurisdiction over that camp, Regular Army or SS. "Army," he said. Now I knew what I had to do. I headed back to the city to find Army headquarters.

All the months I had worked for the SS stood me in good stead now. I knew more about the military and how it worked than most soldiers. I knew what to ask, whom to ask, and how to ask. An ordinary civilian could spend days running from one office to another, but I had everything I needed to know in five minutes. Once I located Army headquarters, I asked one of the soldiers coming out who the officer in charge of the labor detention camps was. Major

Bauer, he told me. I took that information around to the main entrance, where I told the sentry on duty that I had an appointment at nine o'clock that morning with Major Bauer.

"That's fine," he said. "But I can't let you in now. It's too early. The offices don't open till nine."

"I understand. But I've come all the way from Kraków for this appointment. The train got in early. It's so cold out here. Could I at least wait inside?"

He relented and directed me to a guardroom, where I could sit until the offices opened. I waited there until nine, then went upstairs to the major's office. A Polish civilian was sitting at the receptionist's desk. I guessed he was the major's secretary.

"I'd like a word with you, if I may," I said to him. "I've come all the way from Kraków. I'd like to see the major."

"About what?"

"About a friend of mine who's being held in that camp ouside the city."

He shook his head. "Those people are needed in Germany, and that's where they're going."

"Wait! I'm not finished. My friend isn't trying to get out of anything. She already has a job in Kraków working for the SS." He still refused to listen. I continued, lowering my voice. "There's something else I think you should know. She fought in the Warsaw uprising and went through hell. As one patriot to another, don't you think she deserves a break?"

"Go away! Save your breath! I can't do a thing for you!" He threw up his hands. "I don't even want to talk to you anymore!"

He was very stubborn, but I can be stubborn, too. "I understand your not wanting to discuss it in the office. Let's get together privately where we can talk. I still have plenty to say. When do you go to lunch?"

"I don't go to lunch."

"Is that so? Or maybe you just don't want to tell me when you go to lunch? Very well. I have nothing else to do. I'll sit here and wait. When you get up to leave the office, I'll follow. I'll stick to you like a burr until I get the chance to say everything I have to say."

Seeing that I wasn't easily gotten rid of, he finally admitted he went to lunch at twelve-thirty. I said I would see him then. But I didn't trust him. He was just the type to try and sneak out ahead of time. I went back downstairs to the guardroom and asked the sentry if I could wait there, explaining that the major still hadn't arrived. He shrugged and let me in. I took a seat by a window overlooking the entrance to the building where I could see everyone going in or out. There was no way for that secretary to slip by me now. I waited several hours. Then I saw him. He came down the stairs with his head down and quickly stepped outside. I ran out and followed him down the street for a quarter of a block before catching up to him. He turned around when he heard me coming.

"Go away! Why are you bothering me? I don't want to talk to you!"

"And I don't want to talk to you either. All I want is an appointment with the major."

'When do you want it?"

"This afternoon."

"This afternoon? You're crazy! You have to wait three days for an appointment."

"Come on, don't give me a hard time! I don't have three days. I have to get back to Kraków tomorrow. Those other people live here. They can come back in three days if they have to, but I can't. Just fit me in somewhere. You know you can do it."

He still refused. I couldn't believe it! I started talking about the uprising again, hoping to play on his patriotic feelings. I got nowhere.

"Okay. I'm not finished yet, but there's no point standing here arguing in the middle of the street. Why don't we go to wherever it is you have lunch? Have a drink on me, and we'll talk some more. What do you say? A glass of vodka?"

"I never drink during working hours."

"Well, how about if I fix it so you can drink when you're not working?"

In the end I got my appointment, and all it cost me was a bottle of vodka. Everything worked out perfectly. The major showed me into his office and listened politely while I explained the situation. I showed him my papers and Colonel Roemer's letter to back up my story. "Besides," I added as I finished, "it isn't as if my friend Irena were trying to get out of contributing to the war effort. We really need her in the infirmary because our other nurses are always being transferred. How often do you find someone who is qualified, experienced, and speaks German? You can always haul someone off the street and make him a factory worker, but how often do you find someone with the qualifications to be a good nurse? Don't you think my friend would be more useful serving as a nurse in Kraków than standing on some assembly line in Germany?"

The major agreed. He had his secretary write out an order for Renia's immediate release. By now it was four o'clock and starting to get dark, so he summoned a messenger to escort me out to the camp. The messenger turned out to be a young Polish man about my age, blond and very handsome.

"Where are you from?" he asked as we started out.

"Kraków."

"Really? I'm from Lwów myself, but I've lived in Częstochowa two years. It's a nice place."

"Yes, it seems like a nice city. I'm sorry I can't stay a while."

"Well, maybe you can come back some other time." We continued walking. Then he said, "I couldn't help notice the name on these release papers. Irena Zaporowska, isn't it? I know Irena Zaporowska."

"Really?"

"Oh, yes! We had a Christmas party out in the camp a few days ago, and I danced with her a couple of times. She's nice. Very intelligent."

I didn't reply. I wasn't sure where this conversation was leading and didn't want to be linked too closely to Renia in case anything went wrong.

"Do you know her identity card is a hundred percent fake?"

Now I had to be very careful. "Really?"

"Oh, yes. It's true. I used to live in Warsaw, so I know the city pretty well. When I saw the address on her card, I knew at once. There's no such house number on that street."

I stopped and looked him right in the eye. "I don't know a thing about that, but I do know this: we're all Poles, and in these hard times we had all better stick together. I don't care if her identity card is forged. It's not my business where she's really from or what her real name is. I was sent up here to get her out of that camp so she can go to work as a nurse in Kraków. That's all I know. That's all I want to know. Life is tough enough without people making trouble for each other."

He didn't say anything further. We walked the rest of the way in silence.

But bad luck was dogging my footsteps. By the time we got to the camp the office was closed, so Renia's release had to wait for the following morning. The messenger returned to Częstochowa with the release order. But I wasn't ready to go back, at least not yet. I asked the guard if it was possible to speak with one of the detainees.

"Who?"

"Irena Zaporowska."

"Go around to the fence, and I'll call her."

I went outside to the barbed wire, and soon Renia came out on the other side to meet me. She was overjoyed to see me. I told her not to worry. Everything was set for her release tomorrow morning. Once she got out, we'd leave for Kraków together.

As long as you're here and everything is under control, I don't mind waiting another night," she said. "But Ruszka, what about you? Do you have a place to stay?"

I told her about the woman I had met at the railway station the night before. I planned to go back to her apartment. Renia did not like that idea.

"Why walk all the way back to the city? It's dark already, and it will soon be curfew. Spend the night here. People do it all the time." She went on to explain that some of the camp guards were Ukrainian auxiliaries who could be bribed to look the other way while a friend or relative of one of the detainees slipped inside. It so happened that one of those guards was on duty that night. Renia went back inside to arrange the deal. We worked it out for a bottle of vodka and a few packs of cigarettes.

I had never been inside a camp before, and even though I was just a visitor, the experience of hearing the gate clang shut behind me and looking out through the barbed wire was unnerving. The barracks where the women detainees slept was a long room with two rows of three-tiered bunk beds separated only by a narrow aisle. There were no mattresses. The beds were wooden boxes filled with straw. Renia was in the third bunk, the one at the top. I took off my shoes and coat and carefully folded my skirt before climbing up. Lying together in the straw, speaking in whispers, Renia told me about Mayer and my father, about the final liquidation of the Piotrków ghetto and how she ran away. She told me about Franka, who had come to the camp several times to see if she could help. But what could Franka do? I was the one with connections, and until I appeared, Renia lived from moment to moment, aware of the other girls' suspicions and knowing she could be betrayed at any time. She described her relief upon returning from the trenches to find the note I left for her. "Thank God!" she told everyone. "My friend Wanda has come from Kraków at last to get me out!"

I winced. Coming straight from the ghetto, Renia didn't know better. But I had been around Polish women long enough to know how their minds worked. "So her friend from Kraków is here to spring her, eh? Is this dirty Jew going to walk out of here while we get shipped to Germany? No way!" I knew we were bound to have trouble. I just prayed nothing would happen until morning.

It was 9:00 P.M. Renia and I were lying in the bunk still talking, when I suddenly heard someone call my name.

"Wanda Gajda! Wanda Gajda!"

The voice was loud and insolent. I knew instinctively that something was wrong.

"Wanda Gajda!"

"Here I am," I answered calmly, as if I had nothing to be afraid of. "Just a minute."

I took my time. Climbing down from the bunk, I got dressed, put on my shoes, and adjusted my skirt. Then I put on my coat, combed my hair, powdered my face, dabbed on a touch of lipstick, and arranged my hat at the perfect angle. If this was to be a confrontation, I wanted to look my best.

Only when I was ready did I start walking toward the corridor. Renia went with me. He was still yelling for Wanda Gajda when we came out: a drab little Polish man in shabby civilian clothes.

"I'm Wanda Gajda," I said to him. "What do you want?"

"I want to talk with you. Come with me." He turned to Renia. "You, go back!" Detainees were allowed only as far as the corridor.

I walked with him to the waiting room outside. There was trouble all right, and I knew exactly what it was. The papers were all in order, and Renia's release was scheduled for the morning. This man wouldn't dare make trouble, wouldn't dare use that tone of voice to someone from an obviously higher social class, unless he suspected I was a Jew. I had to be. My friend Zaporowska was obviously a Jew, and if I had taken the trouble to come all the way from Kraków to get her out, then it was a sure bet I was Jewish myself. I saw the game right away. He was trying to scare me, hoping I'd panic and try to bribe him. But I don't scare easily.

"I know who you are."

"Really?" I replied in my haughtiest tone. "I'm sorry, but I don't recall ever having had the *pleasure* of meeting you."

"You're not Wanda Gajda. I know you. I've seen you somewhere before."

I walked over to the hall light, took off my hat, and held my head high so that the light was shining directly on my face.

"Now take a good look," I said. "Are you sure you know me? That would be very surprising because I know I've never seen you before. I'm from Kraków. This is my first time in Częstochowa. Were you ever in Kraków?"

"No, but I know you," he kept insisting. "I know you."

"Well, what can I say? Maybe you don't see right. Maybe you need glasses." I showed no sign of being concerned at all. Finally he gave up arguing and told me to follow him. He took me down a dark corridor to an office reserved for German camp personnel. A soldier was sitting at the desk.

"*Sie Jude!*" he shouted to the soldier, pointing his finger at me. "*Jude, Jude, Jude!*"

He was trying to tell the soldier that I was Jewish, to arrest me. But as soon as I heard him trying to speak German, I realized that he probably didn't know more than those two words. His accent was so poor it was hard to understand what he was saying. *Jude* is pronounced "Yoo-duh," not "Yew-deh," the way he was saying it. I might have been in trouble, but I had one advantage. I spoke German. My accuser did not. I intended to play that card for all it was worth.

"What? What are you saying?" The soldier didn't understand him at all.

The man started waving his arms and yelling. "*Sie . . . nicht Wanda Gajda! Sie Yew-deh! Yew-deh, Yew-deh, Yew-deh! Zaporowska . . . Sie Yew-deh!*" He was trying to tell him that I wasn't really Wanda Gajda, that I was a Jew who had come to get her friend Zaporowska, another Jew, out of the camp.

The German sighed and asked to see my passport. I handed it over without hesitation. He began reading out loud: "Wanda Regina Gajda . . . Aryan . . . Roman Catholic . . . Address . . . " He shrugged, folded the document, and handed it back "Does he think you're Jewish because your middle name is Regina?" He still had no idea what this was all about.

"Who knows?" I replied. "I'm not Jewish. I'm Polish. I'm employed by the Third SS Pioneer Training Battalion in Kraków. I work for the Kommandant, Colonel Roemer, as a nursemaid. I've lived with him and his wife for the last two years. If you don't believe me, here is his military telephone number. I'll wait here until the call goes through. You ask Colonel or Mrs. Roemer if I'm Jewish or not." Then I started showing him my papers. I had reams of them by this time, all genuine. I showed him my work card, my identity card, my ration card, my residence permit, my passport, my baptismal certificate, my pass to enter the barracks. I even showed him my special pass to walk the dog after curfew. "I still don't understand why he thinks I'm Jewish," I said when I finally finished showing him all my documents.

But that horrid little man kept yelling, "*Nein, nein! Sie Yew-deh! Yew-deh, Yew-deh, Yew-deh, Yew-deh!*"

Then I took out my special permit to get on the train. "Now look at this. Do you see what it says here? 'The Pole, Wanda Gajda, has permission to travel . . . ' It doesn't say 'The Jew.' What more do you want from me? I've shown you all my papers. I've even given you a telephone number to call. Why don't you call? Whom do you believe? This civilian who can hardly speak two words of German, or your own officers in the SS? Come on, now. Whom do you believe?"

The soldier held his head in his hands a moment, pondering the situation. "You certainly are right, I have no question about these documents. But could you please wait outside in the corridor a moment. I'd like a word with this fellow."

I went outside. As I waited, I heard them arguing in the office but couldn't make out what they were saying. Suddenly another door opened, and an army captain entered the hallway. He was quite surprised to see me and took a step back.

"What in the world is such a lovely young lady doing here so late in the evening?"

I turned to him at once. "Sir, I'm having a problem. Can you help me?" Before he quite got over his surprise, I told him my entire story, closing with " . . . but then this one little man accused me of being Jewish. I know what he wants. He wants a bribe. If I don't pay him, he'll make trouble for me."

"We'll see about that!" the captain exclaimed. "Please follow me."

We went into the office. My papers were still spread over the desk. "What's going on here?" the captain asked in a very stern voice.

"This one says she's Jewish . . ." the soldier started saying, but the captain cut him off.

"Nonsense! Throw him out!"

The soldier grabbed the little man by the collar and booted him out the door. Then the captain invited me to sit down, apologizing profusely for all the trouble and embarrassment I had been caused. He gathered up all my papers, folded them carefully, and handed them back. I was anxious to leave while everything was still in my favor, but at the same time I couldn't seem too eager to go. So I chatted awhile with the captain. He asked me about my job.

"Tell me, who is this Kommandant you work for?"

"Do you know Colonel Roemer? He commands the Third SS Pioneer Training Battalion."

"Oh? I thought the Third was in Prague."

If that question was loaded, it didn't work. I knew all about the SS. "No. The First is in Prague. The Third is in Kraków." I also knew that the Regular Army was intensely jealous of the SS, which received better rations, better quarters, and all sorts of extras. So when the captain asked "What is it like to work for the SS? Is it as good as they say?" I knew exactly how to answer.

"It's better. The rations are terrific, and they also get R-6 cigarettes."

"R-6? Really? I'd give a month's pay for an R-6 cigarette right now!"

I laughed. "Why didn't you say so?" I took out my cigarette box and gave him the whole pack. At first he wouldn't take it, but I insisted. "Go ahead. It's yours. After all, you did me a big favor."

By then it was ten-thirty and time to go. I thanked the captain for his help, shook hands, and walked very slowly out the door and through the main gate. My face was nonchalant, but my heart was pounding.

It was dark and very late, and I still had no place to stay. Earlier Renia had told me that Franka had taken an apartment in Częstochowa, but that was the last place I wanted to go. Tonight was no time to be near anyone Jewish. I walked slowly back toward the city, wondering what to do. On the way I passed a woman with two small children. I stopped and explained my problem.

"I just came from visiting my friend in the camp. My train leaves at four-thirty, and I know I won't be able to get to the station before curfew. Could I sit up in your house for a few hours? I'd be glad to pay."

She told me not to bother; I could sit in her kitchen for free. We went to her house, had some tea, and talked. Then the woman went to bed while I sat up thinking about what to do. I realized that there was no point in going back to the camp. The messenger was coming with the papers in the morning, and the captain had promised to take care of Renia's release personally. Time was getting short, and I had to be back in Kraków by the thirtieth to help Mrs. Roemer. When morning came, instead of returning to the camp, I continued to the railway station to catch the next train home. I expected Renia to follow shortly.

But Renia never did come to Kraków. After I left that night, the captain came by to talk to her.

"You know, your friend Wanda is charming," he said. "I enjoyed talking with her very much. She's very nice."

Renia didn't want to appear too nervous, so she merely asked, "Could you send her back here for a while? I haven't seen her in so long. We have a lot to talk about, and we didn't get a chance to finish."

"I'm afraid I can't," he apologized. "You see, she's gone. I imagine she's probably on her way back to Kraków by now." That was all Renia needed to hear. At least she knew I wasn't under arrest.

The next day something was missing—stolen, most likely—and no one was let out. Renia had to wait until the day after, when the messenger from headquarters showed up with the order for her release. The officer on duty was going through her file, examining her papers, when he suddenly said, "I see you're going to go to work for the SS. I hope you realize that the Army could use some qualified people, too. In fact, I could give you a job right now. We need another cook in the officers' mess. But I guess you think the SS is classier than the Army."

Renia thought it over. This was a good offer. In exchange for a little work cleaning and cooking for the officers, she'd have food and housing, and wouldn't have to face the dangers of the long railway trip to Kraków. She remembered what I told her about life on the outside. She decided to accept.

Two weeks later the Russians crossed the Vistula, the Germans were in full retreat, and she was free.

By then so was I.

An End . . .
and a
Beginning

Finally it came. In January the Russians crossed the Vistula. They drove straight for Kraków. The Germans couldn't hold them back. Colonel Roemer came and went at all hours. Sometimes we didn't see him for days, but the telephone, hooked up to the military line, rang constantly. Whenever I picked up the receiver, there was an officer on the other end of the line demanding to speak to Colonel Roemer. The message was always urgent. Meanwhile the *Krakauer Zeitung* was still prattling about "straightening out the lines," except now, in order to straighten them, it was necessary to evacuate Kraków. Mrs. Roemer and Klaus were leaving for Magdeburg again. This time I knew they wouldn't be back.

"Wanda, we will not leave you behind for the communists," Mrs. Roemer promised me just before she got on the train. She had her husband swear to take me with him when the time came. Meantime, I was to remain behind in the apartment and look after the furniture.

What furniture it was! Colonel Roemer was a brutal man, but he had exquisite taste. That furniture was his most valued possession. I can almost believe he fought the war for it. It came from a special SS warehouse filled with valuables stolen from Jewish homes. High-ranking officers with apartments to furnish could help themselves. The Roemers' bedroom and living-room suites were inlaid with intricate parqueted patterns and covered with rare veneers. A sumptuous Oriental rug and a graceful sofa highlighted the living room. But it was the dining-room set that was Colonel Roemer's special pride. The three-hundred-year-old ebony table and chairs were elaborately carved with different mythological scenes. The buffet was ten feet long and just as magnificent. But the wine cabinet was the prize, covered from top to bottom with carved grape vines framing episodes from the life of Bacchus.

Like all other senior officers, Colonel Roemer made plans to haul his loot back to Germany. I was a part of that booty because a Fräulein Wanda was as rare a find as the dining-room furniture. I suppose I should have been flattered, but I was far from happy about it. I didn't want to go to Germany. That was the last place I wanted to be. When the Russians came to Kraków—and by now it was obvious they would be there soon—I wanted to be there to meet them.

An End . . . and a Beginning

215

The battle for Kraków raged. Toward the east the sound of heavy artillery rumbled in the distance like summer thunder. Each day the battle lines drew closer and closer to the city as the German Army fell back. Colonel Roemer was constantly in the field. He came home only to rest, bathe, and change his clothes before leaving for his office again. He once held a staff meeting in the apartment. From the faces of the officers present I knew that the situation must be very grave. Roemer himself looked physically and emotionally exhausted. Before he left he called me aside and told me to have my bags packed. Should it become necessary for him and his staff to evacuate Kraków, he had left orders that I was to be taken with them. As he promised his wife, he was not going to leave me behind for the Russians.

That night the Russians shelled the city. Everyone in the apartment house ran for shelter in the basement. I was nearly out the door when the telephone rang. I was about to go back to pick it up when an inner voice warned me not to answer. Colonel Roemer had promised to take me back to Germany with him. I knew that call had something to do with that. I left the phone ringing as I hurried downstairs to the cellar.

I found all the neighbors down there, some on the verge of panic, others calm, listening to the shells exploding in the distance. Suddenly we heard voices and an urgent pounding on the front door. The janitress was about to go up to see who it was, but I begged her to stay downstairs. "Don't open it!" I pleaded. "Those are soldiers sent to get me. Colonel Roemer wants to take me back to Germany with him, but I don't want to go." She stayed where she was. The pounding on the door continued for what seemed like hours. Then it stopped.

We spent that night huddled in the cellar as shellfire rattled the walls of the apartment house above us. All night long we heard the tramp of marching boots, the rumble of tanks and heavy vehicles.

Morning came to us in silence. The world was absolutely still. Quietly we crept up from the cellar and peered out into the street. The only German in sight was a soldier sprawled on the pavement, killed by a piece of shrapnel. One by one we stepped outside, then slowly, carefully ventured a little farther up the block. Could it be true? Were they really gone? After five long, bitter years, were we finally free?

Others were emerging from the cellars now, cautiously at first, then boldly, joyfully as they realized there was nothing to fear. Groups of young people darted here and there gathering abandoned weapons, then running off to join in the sporadic shooting still continuing in other parts of the city.

"Let's go downtown and see what's happening," a girl said to me. I never saw her before, but now there were no strangers. Off we went. We arrived downtown to find hundreds of people milling about in the streets in joyous confusion. We joined the throng. Suddenly shots rang out. Everyone scattered. We ended up in a convent basement with a crowd of other thrill seekers waiting for the gunfire to subside. It went on all night.

By morning we were tired of sitting in basements. Shooting or not, we poured out into the streets. The whole population of Kraków was converging on the downtown area. Crowds smashed in the windows of liquor stores and began passing out bottles of champagne. Soon geysers of champagne were raining down in torrents. Everyone had an open bottle in his hand. We sang and cheered and

An End . . . and a Beginning

217

laughed and danced. Fighting was still going on. A single shell could have blown us all to bits, but no one cared. It was over now. The bitter years of slavery and death were at an end.

The next day the Red Army entered the city. Enormous tanks came rumbling up the streets with young soldiers riding on top waving flags and rifles and shouting in Polish and Russian, "Hurrah for victory! Hurrah for Stalin! Russians and Poles, brothers forever!" And Poles, who normally despise Russians and hate communists, were there by the thousands cheering them, kissing them, carrying them on their shoulders. And I was there too, right in the middle of the crowd, screaming, laughing, shouting with the rest. "Hurrah for freedom! Hurrah for the Soviet Union! Hurrah for the Red Army!" Years of bottled-up tension and fear came pouring out in an avalanche of hysterical emotion. Total joy! Total freedom! The world was beautiful.

It didn't last. When I dragged myself wearily home after screaming my voice out for hours, I found the neighbors waiting for me. I never had much to do with the people in the neighborhood before, but they knew that I worked for Colonel Roemer and that I made frequent visits to the barracks. Now that the Germans were gone, they wanted first pick of the loot.

"You know where the supply rooms are," they said. "We can't waste time looking around. We want you to lead us to them."

I cared nothing for the battalion's property, but the glittering, eager look in their eyes disgusted me. Like a flock of vultures, each had come with his box or sack to pick the bones clean. But I didn't have a choice. I wasn't about to refuse a mob.

I led them to the supply stores and showed them where

the cigarettes and the boots and the uniforms and the liquor were kept. The doors were locked, but someone found the keys. Word spread through the neighborhood like a brush fire, and within minutes a huge mob had gathered to fight for the booty.

I wanted no part of looting. I left and returned home. On the way I ran into an old woman who lived downstairs. "Wanda?" she said, surprised to see me coming back empty-handed. "Didn't you get anything?"

I realized that I ought to go back and pick up something just for appearance's sake. I returned and managed to come away with several boxes of cigarettes. In the first tumultuous days of liberation these turned out to be my working capital.

Colonel Roemer was gone, but his presence hung over the apartment like a dark cloud. His furniture was all in place. His collection of rare wines and brandies still lined the liquor cabinet. His pistols rested in well-oiled holsters, while from its customary hook in the hallway his black leather coat waited like a hobgoblin for its master's return.

One day a boy who had worked at the barracks appeared at the door. "What do you want?" I asked. He told me he had come for Colonel Roemer's furniture. He was going to take it for himself.

"You go to hell!" I shouted. "I worked here, not you. If this stuff belongs to anyone, it belongs to me!" Eventually he gave up and left, but I knew that wasn't the end of it. The vultures were gathering. He'd be back.

Sure enough, he showed up again a few days later, but this time he had a Russian officer with him. The Russian had taken an apartment nearby and was going to furnish it with Colonel Roemer's furniture. By now I realized there was no

An End . . . and a Beginning

219

point in fighting the inevitable. Hadn't the Germans furnished their homes with loot? The Russians were only doing the same. To the victor belong the spoils. But at the same time I saw no reason why I should allow them to take everything. I was entitled to my share, too. So we worked out a compromise. They took the larger pieces while I kept the smaller ones, which were really all I needed to furnish a place of my own.

After we arranged the deal, the Russian strolled through the apartment opening drawers and closets, examining whatever struck his fancy. Before he left he noticed the black leather coat hanging in the hallway. He took it with him on his way out. Then, with the quiet clicking of the latch and the fading echo of footsteps down the hall, the last vestige of the Colonel Roemer passed from my life forever.

Only one task remained. I had to go back to Piotrków. I had to return to the city of my childhood: to my house, to my courtyard, to my street. It was the only way of putting a seal on my past. I had to see it once more to know that it was really gone.

And so I went back to Piotrków, to the Judengasse, the old Jewish section of the city. As I walked through the empty cobbled streets, I remembered what they were like ages ago, before the war. I remembered the perpetual crowds that filled the shops, the courtyards, the market stalls, the tiny one-room synagogues. The whole district pulsed with life. Now these same streets were deserted. The only sound was the echo of my footsteps . . . that and the sigh of the wind.

In the courtyards mountainous heaps of trash lay piled like debris in the wake of a natural disaster. Everywhere I looked I could see the ragged remnants of clothing and bedding intermingled with fragments of furniture. So much dirt, sand, and garbage had been tossed on top of the rubbish heaps that they were now as high as small hills. At the very top of one, precariously but impudently perched, I glimpsed a broken white chamber pot.

I walked on, past the boarded-up stores, the abandoned apartments. It was like walking through a graveyard. Heaps of dirt and rags were all that remained of a vibrant, living community.

I came to the courtyard where the poorhouse, the *Bays Lekhem*, stood. I remembered how the volunteers used to make their rounds through the courtyards on Saturdays, carrying their big laundry baskets, crying *"Bays Lekhem! Bays Lekhem!"* My mother and the other women would always throw down an extra challah or, at the very least, a piece of bread so the poor would have something for their sabbath meal. Now an old Polish woman was sitting in front of the building holding a little boy on her knees. His only garment was a shirt that barely reached his navel. He wriggled as the woman searched his head for lice.

It was all so quiet. The very silence brought to mind a poem I once read called "Silence in Europe."

It's quiet in Europe now.
We don't have those noisy Jews around anymore . . .

I had seen enough. I was ready to leave. But there were still two places to visit. One was Mayer's house. I found the building where the Zarnowieckis used to have their store. I opened the door, and a little bell rang—the same little bell I remembered. The fixtures in the store were the same, too, though they had been moved from their original places. The shelves were bare. I had no idea what the people

An End . . . and a Beginning

221

were selling. A Polish woman came out from the back and asked what I wanted. I asked if she had a comb. No, she didn't have one. I stole a quick glance into the back room as she left, but there was nothing to see. I went out and walked around back to the courtyard, but there was nothing there either. I continued on to my house.

Eleven steps led up to our door. The tenth step was loose. It had been loose for as long as I could remember. As I climbed those steps now, I stopped on the tenth one. It still wasn't fixed. How strange, I thought. So many changes —in the world . . . in me—but these steps hadn't changed at all. The tenth step was still loose.

I knocked at the door. A woman opened it. Quickly I planted my foot inside the door so she couldn't shut it before I was ready. I had to see my home once more. I had to see the rooms where my family lived, the little house where I grew up. But all was gone. Everything had changed. The floor wasn't red. The furniture wasn't the same. Nothing was as I remembered it. Then I turned to the woman and realized to my shock that I knew her. Her husband was a railroad engineer. She was a friend of my parents'. But she didn't recognize me, and I kept my identity to myself. I asked if Tony lived there, but she told me no, there was no one there by that name. I heard her lock the door behind me as I walked down the stairs. As I turned into the courtyard for the last time, I looked back to see if my mother's crocheted curtains still hung in the window. If they did, I was prepared to go back and pay any price for them just to have something from my mother's hands. But the curtains were gone.

Then for one long moment I stood in the empty courtyard where I had taken my first step, where I and my friends had gathered to ponder the mysteries of algebra and geography, where we dreamed about the future and planned the building of a better world.

It was time to go. The train would be coming in soon, and I had a long walk back to the railway station. I'd catch the night train and arrive in Kraków by morning. I knew I had a lot to do. I had to find an apartment and move my furniture. It was important to get everything set up as soon as possible because, after all, my brother would be coming back . . . and maybe Mayer . . . and my father . . . and possibly even my little sister Pola, if she had been lucky and someone had been kind to her. Yes. Some would surely be coming back. And when they did, they would need a place to stay and someone to look after them. There wasn't much time. I had to get ready. There was a lot of work to do . . .
Tomorrow.

An End . . . and a Beginning

Epilogue

*Benek survived the war as a Polish worker in Germany.
He now lives in Chicago. He has two children and two
grandchildren.*

Renia Zaks lives in Haifa.

*Rose's (Wanda's) father died in 1944 in Blizin, a sub-
camp of Auschwitz. Rose's mother and sister Pola were
taken to Treblinka. Of the 750,000 Jews transported to this
camp, only 50 survived.*

*Colonel Roemer was killed in the fighting before
Prague. His wife and son are living in Germany.*

*Mayer, Rose's fiancé, was a prisoner in Buchenwald,
Sliben, and Theresienstadt concentration camps. He and*

Rose were married in 1945. They helped smuggle 135 Jewish children out of Soviet-occupied Poland before settling in Germany in the American Zone. For the next five years they served as head educators in a home for Jewish refugee children in Lindenfels. They came to the United States in 1951. Since that time they have lived in South Bend, Indiana. They have three children and one grandchild.